"Beyond the Red Gauntlet"

Anne Bill

Edited by B A Foster & Nicola Verner
Designed by Chris McClenaghan

AB Publications
Belfast

Published by: Anne Bill, 2002

Text Copyright © 2002 Anne Bill

Photographs Copyright © Various Photographers
- details on application to Publisher

Cover Design Copyright ©
Chris McClenaghan/Anne Bill

ISBN - printed edition 0-9543524-0-8

ISBN - net version 0-9543524-1-6

All Rights Reserved

Printed in Northern Ireland

Acknowledgements

I wish to acknowledge all those who have went out of their way to play a part in the writing of this book through their assistance, support and personal contributions

Mark Coulter – Voluntary Community Worker – Research Information & Photographs

John Macvicar - Research Information - Community Development Officer

Stuart McCartney – Community Development Worker

Andy Cooper – Voluntary Community Worker – Research Information

Hugh Megarry – Voluntary Community Worker – Research Information

Trevor – For help with name and research information

Edited by B A Foster & Nicola Verner

Photographs courtesy of a local resident

Cllr Billy Hutchinson MLA, Nigel Dodds MP, Cllr Nelson McCausland and Rev Norman Hamilton who all played their part in supporting me throughout my years in community.

And I wish to acknowledge all those who have went out of their way to play a part in their local community – wherever you are.

*This book is dedicated to the
Community of Upper Ardoyne*

*Who made a stand against all odds for the rights and survival
Of a minority interface community*

And

All those Protestant interfaces in North Belfast who continue to suffer as minority communities under pressure to abandon their homes. Also to all those devoted volunteers who have dedicated their lives through sheer commitment to their community for so long and expected nothing in return.

One very positive factor that has come out of the pain and hurt of the past year is a group called "The North Belfast Women's Initiative and Support Project," who have come together in Upper Ardoyne to address some of the social issues and needs in the area, and to compliment the groups who were already in place.

What must also be addressed to all the members of CRUA, past and present, who voluntarily have against all adversity dedicated literally their heart and souls to trying to find compromise within this deeply divided community "At least we can say we genuinely tried."

Finally to my family, colleagues at work, special friends (who know who you are), neighbours of Upper Ardoyne, who have all given me the courage and support to pursue this to the end, knowing they believed in me and supported the principles which motivated me to write it.

Contents

	Introduction
Chapter 1	The History - Why the siege mentality
Chapter 2	What forces a minority community to make a stand?
Chapter 3	The Writing on the Wall – Greater Glenbryn Community Initiative
Chapter 4	19th June 2001 - The straw that broke the camel's back
Chapter 5	The Ardoyne Road Dispute - A dormant community becomes proactive.
Chapter 6	3rd September 2002 - The mindless decision which prevented dialogue
Chapter 7	Perceptions of an orchestrated media campaign
Chapter 8	The Forgotten Children
Chapter 9	Twaddell Avenue. A sister Interface
Chapter 10	Outcry for Community Safety - The promised package
Chapter 11	Ongoing low key intimidation. The Ongoing Saga
Chapter 12	The uniting of Protestant Interfaces
Chapter 13	The Words of the People
Chapter 14	Letters from the heart.
Chapter 15	Short Quotations
	Authors Note

The Introduction

"Beyond the Red Gauntlet"

Firstly an explanation of the title of this book, Throughout the Ardoyne Road Dispute in 2001 all we heard of was how children and parents of Holy Cross School had to 'run the gauntlet' and the media produced an abundance of tiny red uniforms on their screens and in their newspapers and magazines to flaunt the plight of something they knew nothing about. This ensured the real underlying story of intimidation of a dying community would never be seen. This is the real story – 'Beyond - The Red Gauntlet.'

Once again the contributors to this book find themselves as many have done before them, totally disempowered by the police service of NI/RUC, Local Government, the media and all those who blatantly ignore the obvious unmistakable signs of our past history. I wish to recognise that this is a community's story and I as the author am only the vehicle in which to enlighten those who have been subjected to misconstruing information and I felt in my capacity as a local community worker for over 20 years – that this story in its entirety had to be told.

With escalation of sectarian intimidation on Protestant people, and the growing number of victims affected by this orchestrated campaign of riot situations and public disorder, it is natural to question why? Is their suffering a product of a Republican agenda and the means to cover up and overpower events they do not want publicised. It is my intention that this book will produce the truth and for people to have the ability to make their own judgement on the situations surrounding the Ardoyne Road.

Even then we have a largely naive and impressionable society who constantly go along with or even contribute to the verbal spiel of victim-hood and negativity of republicans. It is always the Protestants fault, they constantly get the blame or more recently like a child with a new word they keep regurgitating "it was the UDA". I have to ask myself why people do not see this. Are they so embroiled and isolated in their own lives that they really do not want to know any more? Is the campaign by the media, PSNI, NIO, NI Executive, Republicans actually working where they disregard the suffering of residents in these areas and class them as troublemakers to appease those who have worked their way into high government positions with the bullet and the gun and have not yet turned their back on terrorism? All of these certainly are the perceptions of numerous Protestants, which I have spoken to, many of whom did not even live in the notorious interface areas of North Belfast but share the feeling of their identity being stripped from them in a meticulous attempt to implement and impose the Good Friday Agreement – no matter the cost.

This is happening all over Northern Ireland but we will specifically speak of the small enclaves of North Belfast especially that of Upper Ardoyne and Twaddell Avenue. These two areas are inextricably linked when it comes to Republican elements in Ardoyne launching their campaign of sectarian intimidation on those residents who refuse to leave their homes.

The perceived bias of the media and policing of the events in Upper Ardoyne in the Summer of 2001 led to Protestant residents in a situation where they felt had no option but to implement their legal right to hold a protest. This was to highlight the seriousness of the ongoing sectarian harassment, intimidation and murder. A brave move considering the world's media and public opinion was against them. Republicans were willing to unjustifiably use young children to mask the ongoing intimidation and harassment they had been inflicting on Protestant residents and endorse their Nationalist agenda. No matter what the cost they were determined to win the sympathies and support of the media and all who watched the broadcasts and were willing to be brainwashed without seeing the truth.
This is the story of a continuing struggle against intimidation of Protestant/Loyalist/Unionist residents and the contribution of the media in exacerbating the constant negligence of truth over the possibility of a "sensationalised media story". Not only did the people of this small area have

to struggle against the intimidation but they also struggled to have their voices heard - that they were neither child abusers nor sectarian thugs but they themselves were undergoing a continuous campaign orchestrated by Republican elements. The purpose of this I hear you ask - to eradicate them from their homes in interface areas. Many times had their Republican neighbours repeatedly warned "We'll be back tonight to burn you out." This behaviour never fully portrayed by the media even though there is video evidence as proof. I certainly recognise that both communities have similar problems and suffer low educational attainment, unemployment, housing issues, anti-social behaviour and crime to name but a few; but why not deal with these serious social issues instead of introducing another problem and a strategy of ethnic cleansing.

This book should clarify the genuine story for those who believe in forming an opinion of their own. To allow an understanding of the life of the Protestant people in North Belfast and the fear they hold for their children, homes and lives. I have included actual quotes from people who live in these areas, who have suffered and from those who took it to the limit and put their reputation, credibility and lives at risk to hold a protest to highlight their plight in an outcry for Community Safety – Something most communities take for granted.

Chapter One

*The History -
Why the siege mentality*

"The Troubles" is a reference to the era of violence and conflict in Northern Ireland beginning with the Civil Rights marches in the late 1960s to the political resolution enshrined in the 1998 Good Friday Agreement. During that time more than 3,000 people were killed, most of them civilians; a significant percentage in North Belfast, But I bear to question the resolution, as thus far there are still communities under siege by aggressors"

The people of Upper Ardoyne are only too aware of the fact that they are under siege from the massive Catholic Ardoyne community. They do not believe at all that every Catholic is out to get rid of them but they know there are elements there that control the ongoing campaign to eradiate them from their homes in the streets earmarked for Republicans. Marked in their history are the facts that principally from 1969 there has been a concerted Republican agenda to rid them from their homes in the area of Ardoyne.

Many of the older population in Upper Ardoyne today, previously lived in the streets of the now exclusively Catholic lower Ardoyne including Cranbrook Gardens, Farrington Gardens, Alliance Avenue and Velsheda Park and can tell the stories of being intimidated, attacked and burnt out of their homes predominately between 1969 and 1971. Even since then the apparent interface has been receding further into the streets where they had already moved to, so endorsing the siege mentality that "they are out to get us out" and "they want our houses".

FLIGHT: A Report on Population Movement in Belfast during August 1971, by John Darby reports:

"Protestant households in North Belfast have evacuated in large numbers from the Farringdon/Cranbrook streets of New Ardoyne."

"A great many Catholic families have found new houses in the New Ardoyne area and in other North Belfast streets off Oldpark Road and Duncairn Gardens formerly occupied by Protestants."

BEYOND THE RED GAUNTLET

North Belfast is notorious for bearing the brunt of many of the sectarian attacks and murders and a realistic problem is that for many working class people in Ardoyne their counterparts across the divide are hurling bricks, bottles, petrol bombs, pipe bombs or shooting at their community. There have been many murders in this small area throughout the reign of the 'troubles', many victims left to live with the pain, hurt and trauma from losing their loved ones and then continuing to be victims in their own homes from the ongoing conflict.

Upper Ardoyne used to be a vibrant, optimistic community where it would have been hard to get a house in the area due to high demand. The properties got older and less adequate to suit the needs of families. It was highlighted on many occasions with Government and the NI Housing Executive itself that here is a real need for family houses in the streets of Upper Ardoyne and especially Glenbryn Park and Drive; but this was ignored and the degeneration of the area continued at an alarming rate giving the perception that people did not want to live there. On many occasions the NIHE have said that there was not a large enough housing list for the area. They refused to accept that people did not want to register for accommodation that was substandard, they wanted a safe, environment to raise their families and in homes that suited the changing needs of the community there.

It has been noted and publicised many times within the media that Republican and Nationalist politicians think that because Protestants moved out of the Glenbryn streets and Berwick road areas that the homes should have been automatically offered to catholic counterparts. They identified the vacant void properties as potential homes for their constituents instead of looking at why the present tenants were moving out, a combination of dilapidated houses and intimidation or was this the strategy to be implemented – Bring the Protestant people to their knees by allowing them to live in substandard housing, forcing them to finally seek adequate housing elsewhere.

Throughout the 30 odd years of the "troubles", the ongoing upsurge of blatant intimidation and sectarian attacks reinforced by low-key terrorization contributed to an exodus out of the area to the outskirts of Belfast. NIO officials have been asked on many occasions to make the area safer by putting security measures in place to help the community to feel safe. Even as far back as this people were crying out for "community safety" and their distress calls were ignored time and time again.

It can be clearly seen that the ongoing expansion of the Ardoyne into the Protestant enclave, the call from Nationalist and Republican politicians for the vacant homes of the fleeing Protestant population, the deterioration and decay of Housing Executive properties in the Upper Ardoyne area and the ongoing intimidation of those living closest to the interface, certainly contributed to the very genuine and valid siege mentality. Certainly a visit to both sides of any interface in North Belfast and possibly now in East Belfast, will be evidence in itself of the indisputable attacks, as many of the Protestant residents have fled their homes in fear for their young families and the rows of unoccupied properties in comparison to the thriving Catholic community speaks volumes. Or so you would think!

The barrage of low key attacks combined with the exodus of Protestant families and the perceived appeasement of Republicans throughout the peace process has led Protestants to feel beleaguered and segregated into a patchwork of small minority communities throughout North Belfast, with common problems throughout them all i.e. lack of facilities, poor housing, low educational attainment, and high unemployment.

These factors may appear to be 'perceived', but no-one wanted to resolve or address those perceptions. Offer a means of listening or changing how the Protestant people felt. Instead the feelings were left to fester – further fuelled by the lack of interest and incidents which were to follow.

Chapter Two

What forces a minority community to make a stand?

We don't have to agree with the actions of this community to honour their commitment, to recognize that the injustices they fought against were real and still prevail today, and to admit that they deserve at least a reluctant portion of understanding and acknowledgement for enduring the horrific years of terrorism lavished on their community.

For the years leading up to the protest in Upper Ardoyne there had been consistent attacks and low-key intimidation that had chipped away at the small community. They were losing many long-standing neighbours who stabilised the once vibrant area. The community infrastructure was at an unbelievable low with practically no financial support from government or peace monies that had been so well accessed by their neighbours. No community workers to develop and address social issues in an area with so much need.

The Protestant people were suffering in silence with many attacks taking place on children and the elderly during daylight hours and ordinary local residents who were coming home in the chilling threat of darkness from a night out of their perceived prison.

One vivid memory is one of a young teenager, just turned 16 years old and starting his first day at a training centre. Again due to no training resources in Upper North Belfast for young people the young man had to go to the nearby Shankill. He went on the morning of 3rd April 2001, two and a half months before the protest, already nervous at this new step to adulthood and future employment, he signed up to his training course. In the afternoon he was heading home early around 2.30pm and got off a bus on the Crumlin Road and proceeded to walk down Hesketh Road (an area in Upper Ardoyne which is occupied by Protestant residents). A white car with 4 grown men pulled up beside the young man. 2 men then got out of the car and started to cruelly beat him, they continued this vicious assault until he fell helplessly to the ground. The other two Republican thugs leaped from the vehicle and joined in the beating as the young man tried to struggle to his feet to flee the aggressors; finally he saw his chance and ran for his life. "I thought I was going to be murdered; they were going to kill me," was the terrified thoughts of this young teenager. You would think that's appalling enough but that is not the end. The young man was so traumatised by this incident that 6 months later he was self medicating on both illicit and prescription drugs to hide the feeling of inadequacy he felt because he could not physically defend himself. Within the next six months he finally was able to access professional help and was under psychiatric care. He was terrified to go out of the house at all. What a waste of a young life - one who wanted to contribute to Northern Ireland's new society but because he was Protestant and lived in Upper Ardoyne he has been left scarred; left to deal with his trauma alone. Authorities' failed to recognise the seriousness of the effects of the attack as they simply turned their heads and ignored the feelings that followed. These feelings will stay with him all of his life. His parent says, "These are our children, who cares about them? Our children have suffered ongoing attacks, but who cares about their safety?"

Most people who live in upper Ardoyne do not go out of the area at night. There are no social activities or venues in the area and many people are frightened of not getting home safely to go elsewhere outside the area. Two years before the protest two family men were coming home from a rare night out at a wedding party. When they reached the Ardoyne Road; a group of young men were pulling off the wooden fences from Protestant homes. The men shouted "leave those peoples houses alone", and actually thought it was young people from Upper Ardoyne. When they drew closer they realised they were wearing Celtic shirts and were actually from the Catholic part of Ardoyne. The young people ran to attack the men; the men were beaten into unconsciousness and could have been murdered only for the response of an elderly resident who called for help. Another two scarred by the sectarian hatred and intimidation. The ambulance which arrived to treat the victims was attacked by the Republicans who shouted "let the bastards die."

Protestant taxi driver Trevor Kell was shot dead in Hesketh Road in Upper Ardoyne on a cold December night coming up to Christmas, out working to make an extra few pounds for his family at Christmas - another innocent victim. A young resident of Hesketh Road ran to help Trevor that awful night and fears she will never get over the trauma of that night and how helpless she felt as the young man died instantly at the scene. After a slight smokescreen from Republicans, the finger of suspicion immediately fell on the IRA; forensic evidence has linked the bullet to an IRA shooting in 1997. The RUC/PSNI blamed Republicans for the death, but could not say that it was planned or carried out by the IRA. A young family left scarred by the sectarian hatred within elements of Ardoyne. Some time later it was reported that two men had been shot by the IRA in Ardoyne, one of which it is believed was questioned over the murder of Trevor. It is suggested that not all of Ardoyne's Republicans are happy with the peace process - and Mr Kell's death was proof of division - division that the IRA quickly dealt with.

Incidents such as the three I have chosen to share above are contributing factors to people being backed into a corner. Feeling their experiences were not being listened to and their need for help being ignored it was inevitable that because they were backed into a corner they would come out fighting.

Daily Mail Article from Jan 12 2002

Government should be aware that they are the inevitable consequence of surrendering to terrorists. If one community sees another getting it's way because of violence, and it's own values and traditions disregarded, it is hardly going to see any point in playing by the rules itself. Also it is rarely reported that many of the children's parents are Republican extremists. If the Government wants order in Ulster, it has to stop giving in to terrorism.

In 1998 a young family moved into their newly decorated home on the Ardoyne Road only three doors from the Ardoyne Road/Alliance Avenue Interface, one of the best houses in the district with plenty of room and gardens at the back and front for the children to play – they were ecstatic at their chance to get one of these houses. Wednesday 4th March 1998, they were at home with their young two year old child. Their home was repeatedly pounded with boulders and rocks as the aggressors shouted, "Burn the orange Bastards out," the little girl (a month before her second birthday) stood the next day with her mother saying "bad man, bang bang." Her Mother said "My child was in convulsions as boulder after boulder hit the door. She was just screaming in terror. I can't put the kids through this anymore; it's the long term effects on them that worry me." " These men were actually staring in my window and one of the ringleaders said 'We know you – your dead, you won't be staying here very long; we're going to burn you out! How can I take the risk with no protection?" These sorts of attack have caused recurring cycles of residents to move out! Those who have registered for homes soon move out again after they take up the tenancy as the blatant attacks start again and the area lose another batch of Protestant residents.

The only way I can explain the effects these attacks have on people is to use an ordinary scenario. If you live beyond an interface, I can understand how you may not be able to contemplate the devastating impact attacks can have. They have become so acceptable and regular that is it easy to shrug them off. However, picture yourself living next door to the 'neighbours from hell'. Constant music, banging all hours of the day and night, feeling intimidated and unable to rationally discuss it with your neighbours, think carefully – I am sure we can all relate to it. Multiply those feelings of frustration, fear, anger and helplessness by 100. Now you have some concept of life on the Ardoyne Road.

This beleaguered community also feel that their identity was and still is being ignored and stripped from them. There was a definite feeling that Protestants had been let down by the "Good Friday Agreement", most felt that the Government was out to appease those who posed the most severe terrorist threat, rather than protect those who felt in genuine danger. In the Good Friday agreement it is said that "all people should live free from sectarian harassment" why then was the Government not listening to the appeals of the Protestant people of Upper Ardoyne (many who voted YES to the promised peace), before they had to proactively go out and protest because no one would pay attention.

What seems to be government strategies and meandering over serious fallacies in the Good Friday Agreement and on the acceptance of certain levels of violence/threats of terror on the nationalist side in caparison with what action has been taken with regards to the loyalist side i.e. incarceration of leading loyalists under the new law of "directing terrorism" and withdrawing the ceasefire from the UDA only spells out to protestants that whatever happens they will be blamed; All ceasefires have been broken but sanctions have only been placed on the loyalist groupings.

In 1997 Greater Glenbryn Community Initiative, a community group in Upper Ardoyne lobbied on behalf of the local community to acquire security gates on the Ardoyne Road due to the ongoing attacks which were well documented, the group insisted on the security measures as long-standing residents of the community were moving out of the area due to ongoing intimidation. The security gates were agreed by the RUC and NIO in principal, until SF declared they did not want the gates on the Ardoyne Road and that they would be objecting to them. All of a sudden the attacks ceased almost immediately and the RUC/NIO reneged on their decision to provide the added security. A local community worker said, "No-one can say that this community did not try to seek their safety and security through the proper channels, they were just ignored when it came to appeasing the whims of SF/IRA" and many I have spoken to have commented that they believe that the NIO have another agenda with regards to Upper Ardoyne – Maybe If they do not provide protection to residents they will move out and that will be rid of another interface. Yet it is blatant that when SF wish to lobby for walls, fences or gates for the protection of residents in Nationalist interfaces i.e. Lanark Way, Short Strand, Mountainview and Newington that it is not challenged by NIO or Government that when it comes to Protestants requesting protection that SF feel it is better to engage in dialogue than build divides – More double standards maybe? What is that infamous line in NI now? - 'Parity of Esteem' – Practice what you preach comes to mind.

The setting up of the Parades Commission did nothing other than make people feel that they were out to ban or re-route marches which were certainly a massive part of their cultural identity and maybe to some the only identity they had or at least had known. This was seen to be used by Republicans to be a baton to beat Protestants with where they are accused of being sectarian marches. Yet a Republican politician, Gerry Kelly SF MLA, is reported on a local news station saying about Ardoyne shop fronts, "***this is a catholic area, they have no right to come through here,***" a sectarian stance if ever I heard one, and does nothing to encourage community dialogue or cross community bonding, in fact it creates a no-go area for Protestants.

Due to the fact that statements such as this have been made, on many occasions, the parents of children in the local Wheatfield Primary School cannot allow their offspring to attend the local library which is also situated in Ardoyne. As part of the children's education they visited the Ardoyne Library regularly in the past but now even the children have stated they would be frightened to go down to Ardoyne for the use of this public facility. One local parent spoke of their fears for the children, "fears are rubbing off on our children as they are now aware of the 'no-go area' past Ardoyne, I asked my child if they would want to use the library with the school but he said "*No we cant go there*" – for gods sake my child is only 8 years old".

Residents in Upper Ardoyne feel they have no right of access to the local shops at Ardoyne and in fact there have been reported ongoing attacks on senior citizens and residents who try to use the shops or local post office. When speaking to residents who have used the shops in the past they all spoke of the fears they have in walking down the Ardoyne Road to the shops and the fears of even driving down the road in the car to use the shopping facilities there. It has been reported lately that shops at Ardoyne are contemplating closure due to the lack of business from the Upper Ardoyne community and their fall in profits. Evidence that the bare-faced sectarianism that is manifesting itself here is affecting both communities

One elderly resident said," *I have been assaulted three times now when I have went down to collect my weekly pension, the first time I did not think anyone would have a problem with me but and I should have known the second time, But I just got up that morning and fell into my normal routine which would have been to go down the Ardoyne Road to the local post office, I only realised I was at risk again when a woman pulled me by the shoulder and swung me round as she said "you are not welcome here, now f**k off you orange bastard", everyone was looking at me and I didn't know what to do, I tried to make my way to a local bus stop to get me away quickly and take me to another post office to collect my money. I was absolutely petrified as a crowd began to gather, I couldn't believe someone would hate me that much I am over 70 years old. What threat am I to anyone?"* The third time, *"I have to go to the Everton Centre to get my medication and I went down one day it was raining cats and dogs, I was frightened but I needed the medication. I went with my umbrella close to my head to get to the chemist to get my tablets; a young teenage girl came over to me and said, "Get out of here you! Or I will break your jaw," I will never go down again; the man from the chemist says he will deliver my medication out to me.*

This is indicative of other resident's accounts of trying to use the shopping facilities at Ardoyne. Again nothing has been done by the Government or the PSNI in relation to ensuring access and safety to use public facilities or to provide alternatives in the Upper Ardoyne community itself, in fact individual PSNI Officers have said that they would advise residents for their own safety not to go down to Ardoyne Shop Fronts.

Excerpts from: A report by the Mapping the Spaces of Fear Research Team at the University of Ulster
– Executive Summary (2000)

The majority of people living in Ardoyne and Upper Ardoyne undertake avoidance strategies which are influenced by fear

The number of people who did and presently do work in mixed workplaces has fallen from 75% to 33%

The community in Upper Ardoyne is more conscious of living in an interfaced area than is the case in Ardoyne. In comparison, the community in Ardoyne feels more besieged in relation to the wider geography of Belfast

Only 1 in 5 respondents from Upper Ardoyne shop within the Ardoyne area. The majority of those who do are elderly and do not own cars. In terms of weekly shopping respondents from both areas generally avail of shopping centres in either Catholic/Nationalist or Protestant/Unionist areas. In sum, 76% of respondents in Ardoyne

- compared to 81.1% in Upper Ardoyne would not shop in places dominated by the other religious/ethnic group
- Women are more fearful than men when walking through their local area at night. The majority of people are afraid of walking through their community at night during the marching season

- Only 17% of men and 3.8% of women would walk through an area dominated by the other religion/ethnic group at night. In upper Ardoyne 60% of respondents compared to 41% from Ardoyne feel threatened when walking through their respective communities at night. Only 11.4% of respondents in Ardoyne compared to 11.4% in Upper Ardoyne would ravel through an area dominated by the other religion.

- Respondents in Ardoyne are 3 times more likely to have been physically attacked outside of their community. Whereas, respondents in Upper Ardoyne are twice as likely to have been physically attacked within their own community

This chapter cannot even begin to outline the indisputable fears, concerns and perceptions of the residents who live in Upper Ardoyne. Added to the above factual information is the ongoing sporadic rioting and attacks, almost nightly confrontations across the 'peace line', cars driving up and down streets eye-balling residents, attacks that have happened when people leave the area to shop and the amount of residents who have had to leave the area due to fear. All these contribute to the ongoing exacerbation of a clearly excessive volatile situation which could lead to nothing other than a reaction at some point where law-biding people who feel frustrated at being ignored by the leaders who profess to represent them and who are elected to do so. Stormont and Westminster are so far from the fraught and besieged streets of Glenbryn. Do they really care about these common communities when they are brushing shoulders with world leaders – the belief is they are making their own people feel insignificant and unrepresented – a cauldron left with all the ingredients to ignite a desperate response when a community reaches the end of its tether.

Chapter 3 Three

The writing on the wall

Contributed by Mark Coulter, Greater Glenbryn Community Initiative

The lack of Community infrastructure led dedicated volunteers to establish community groups to highlight serious concerns about Upper Ardoyne – the most significant being Greater Glenbryn Community Initiative in relation to housing and security – but this should not have been taken by government as an opportunity to shirk their official responsibilities.

I was raised in a quiet area of the Oldpark Road not far form Glenbryn, in a mixed estate where Catholics and Protestants had lived in peace together since before the outbreak of the troubles. As part of a strict Christian upbringing I was taught to be tolerant, not to hate, and whilst I knew there were differences between the Protestant and Catholic faiths, I held fast to the principle that this was no reason to dislike someone of 'the other persuasion'.

Whilst members of my community were being killed in the conflict, I never for one minute thought of pointing the finger at Catholic neighbours around me – after all, many of them moved into the mixed area to avoid seeing their children conscripted into Republican paramilitaries.

Although only a short distance away, I never crossed the doorstep to Glenbryn until I was around 13 years old, and it was obvious that I was in another world. The Alliance Avenue peaceline was riddled with bullet holes, as were the sides of the Protestant homes. The Alliance estate, Alliance Road and Glenbryn were all 100% two-up two-down terraced houses, and although many had fallen into disrepair, people seemed content to keep them as best they could.

It was on my short walks to and from the Glenbryn estate that I had my first of many real encounters of sectarian hatred. One night walking alone through Deerpark to the Oldpark Road, a small group of men lined across the road and tried to hunt me down. I was a keen sports player, small for my age and pretty fast on my feet, but one of them managed to land a blow. He backed off when I defended myself but I saw his friends grab milk bottles and rush towards me, so I made off. One of the crowd was later arrested, and it turned out to be a relative of a local TV celebrity. When the celebrity was condemning sectarianism on his TV appearances, I wondered if he knew what his brother was up to in North Belfast. It wasn't the last time I would experience hatred from people who knew nothing about me other than I had just come out of a Protestant area.

Over the years, I saw Glenbryn deteriorate into a state of complete disrepair, with the Housing Executive seeming to rush in to demolish homes at first opportunity, but never replacing what they took away. Gradually, as promises of new housing went unfulfilled, people who wanted to stay felt they had no choice but to move away if they were to give their children a decent environment in which to grow up.

It was irritating that those with the responsibility of ensuring acceptable living standards were maintained had simply abandoned the area, whilst millions of pounds were being pumped into neighbouring Nationalist areas. I found it hard to understand how this institutionalised neglect could be happening, but soon the penny dropped. People who were prepared to put up with the decay had another headache with which they had to cope. There had been an upsurge in attacks on homes in the Glenbryn and Alliance areas, and coincidentally at the same time, local Sinn Fein Councillors were putting pressure on the Housing Executive to demolish Glenbryn more quickly. One was quoted in the North Belfast News: *'The Housing Executive is not doing enough to demolish Glenbryn to facilitate the expansion of the Nationalist Ardoyne community which is bulging at the seams.'*

So there it was – Protestant families were expected and even pressured into abandoning the area where they were raised, simply to make way for a Nationalist community who didn't see Protestants as neighbours, but an obstacle in the way of a Brit-free North Belfast. When they say 'Brits out', *do they mean me – they surely do!*

I watched as more and more people moved out of the Glenbryn Streets, fed up with having to take their children to hospital after sectarian attacks, fed up with having to get up in the middle of the night to board up the windows, and tired of living under siege where they had to virtually sneak in and sneak out past Nationalist Ardoyne if they wanted to go somewhere else in town.

Eventually in 1996, I couldn't sit and watch any longer. The neglect of the area was a disgrace, and the Government was doing nothing about the nightly attacks, not just petrol-bombings, but when crowds of Republicans would march into the estate and physically kick in the front doors of houses. I gathered support for a community group which we named the Greater Glenbryn Community Initiative. We recorded every attack on homes, cars and people, and eventually submitted the details to the police and Northern Ireland Office. Republican representatives told police that the attacks were not orchestrated, but were down to elements beyond their control. The police were able to confirm every incident, and the Security Minister immediately recommended a peaceline along Alliance Avenue and gates on Ardoyne Road. Suddenly, although Republicans had said they were powerless to intervene, the attacks were switched off like a light-bulb.

Nothing happened, not even a stone was thrown. In the meantime,

Nationalist representatives including Sinn Fein overruled the residents of Alliance Avenue, and did all they could to stall the building of a peaceline. The then local priest, Fr Kenneth Brady, wrote to Holy Cross parishioners saying: '…..I contacted the police and as a result they will not be proceeding with the barrier.' I thought it strange that a priest could overrule an entire community, but it set the scene for the years that followed. After a period of calm, Republicans asked for a review of the situation and of course the police reported 'all quiet'. The decision to build the peaceline was rescinded, and of course the attacks started up again a few months later.

At this time, the old bus depot site was derelict, and the plans to build new houses were submitted. In a nutshell, the go-ahead was given on the condition that the houses backed onto Ardoyne Road, and did not face front-wards onto it, as the road was still at that time considered to be a thoroughfare. The houses were built facing front-wards onto the road anyway. Again, the system overruled by individuals in a community. Oddly enough, the developer of these houses was also a priest!

Eventually, phase 2 of the new houses was built right beside the interface at Ardoyne Road Alliance Avenue. On 26 March 1999, I wrote to elected representatives regarding this development, as follows:

It is outrageous that these additional houses will also face out onto the road as we had heard concerns when this was discussed before, that it will:

Multiply the pedestrian presence in an interface area, consequently multiplying the likelihood of sectarian conflict(remember Mr & Mrs ………..

have already had their windows broken once this month);Completely seal off the lower Ardoyne Road from use by upper Ardoyne Residents, turning the area in to one long gauntlet to be run; Doubtless create the opportunity for a new resident's group to start calling the tunes on issues which affect Protestants immediately beside the interface, such as security presence in the area, interface peaceline measures etc;

*Change the situation of the Everton complex from being in an interface, to being in the heart of a Nationalist residential area, effectively removing it from the reach of the Protestant community, particularly should unrest recur; Psychologically destroy any prospect of ever encouraging Protestant residents to occupy homes on Ardoyne Road immediately above Alliance Avenue. Completely change the complexion of Ardoyne Road right up to and including Hesketh;*Every single item on this list has now happened, but did the planners want to listen? No. Did the Security Minster (Adam Ingram) want to listen? No – he even refused to meet us. Did the Nationalist community think we should be consulted? No! (But try putting a bend in a road without consulting Nationalists – they threaten to execute the builders!)

By this time it was patently clear that not only were we fighting our own social ills, sectarian attacks and economic deprivation, but we were also fighting a Government that did not give a monkeys about anything but keeping Ardoyne Republicans happy.

Over the years we tried to concentrate on bringing forward housing regeneration plans for the Glenbryn area, but were dogged with other problems, including frequent riots at the Ardoyne Road interface. We started spending days and nights on the interface, working along with representatives of

Wheatfield, Alliance, Glenbryn and Ballysillan, getting to the kids before they became drawn in. The kids responded, and I was proud of them. Before long, instead of retaliating when stones were thrown at them, many of them were able to laugh, turn away and get on with their lives whilst the stone-throwers got upset that the Protestant kids were no longer taking the bait.

As I look through the minutes of meetings of our community group, I can see that on nearly every occasion SINCE 1997 there are complaints of Protestant children being chased off the Ardoyne Road by Catholic parents going to and from Holy Cross School, pensioners being abused, cars and homes being damaged. Protestants were taunted as more and more homes in Glenbryn emptied following sectarian attacks. 'Ha ha, only a few streets left. You might as well give us the keys now' they would sneer. On the other hand there were the normal parents going to and from the school. They could look you in the eye to say hello – basically they treated residents like human beings. Unfortunately those who saw Protestants as unwelcome guests occupying homes destined for Nationalists; grew steadily in number.

Yet although these attacks were raised at every meeting, people accepted that because of the presence of ordinary parents and children on the road, they could do little about it but rely on the police to take action. So on a regular basis, meetings took place with the police, and on every occasion for 3 years the answer was the same – 'we are aware of the problems but we don't have the resources to do anything about it.' Eventually in October 2000, after a large number of Protestants had AGAIN moved out of Glenbryn due to the latest concerted round of sectarian attacks, a meeting attended by representatives of most of the interface areas in Oldpark policing area, discussed the issue. I stood up, read a statement, and left the meeting in protest at police inactivity towards the serious situation developing at the Ardoyne interface. Every other representative of Protestant interfaces stood-up, expressed similar views, and left the meeting. This should have been a wake-up call as to the feelings of abandonment and desperation in North Belfast's Protestant communities. But did anyone care?

Trevor Kell was subsequently murdered by the Provisional IRA (on cease-fire!) in Hesketh Road in December 2000. If the warnings at the meeting with the police had been taken seriously, if the Northern Ireland Office had made their own decision regarding the peaceline rather than being dictated to by Nationalists, if someone somewhere had taken even the slightest interest in the warnings, then one life might have been saved. But even now, in the year 2002, the fears and concerns of the Upper Ardoyne people are brushed off with contempt. How many more lives will be lost? How many more families will be made homeless? How many more families will be scarred for life by opening their front door to find an innocent man lying murdered on their doorstep?

Eventually, the inevitable happened in June 2001. Having realised that it was possible to roam the Upper Ardoyne murdering, destroying property and intimidating residents, Republicans launched a large scale assault on Ardoyne Road. Some youngsters were putting up flags on Ardoyne Road when a convoy of cars started to build-up, hidden from sight in Nationalist Alliance Avenue. According to a Catholic resident of Alliance Avenue, some of the faces in the convoy would have been well-known in the area, but not that well-liked. One of the cars drove up whilst the rest waited. The car drove at the youngsters, one of whom was knocked off the ladder. As he struggled to his feet, the passengers jumped from the car, armed with screwdrivers and attacked both him and his friend. As the commotion grew louder, other youths came to assist, and one of them smashed the windscreen of the car with the ladder which had been knocked to the ground a short time before. Then the convoy of waiting cars received the signal to join in, and they sped up the Ardoyne Road, and jumped out of their cars with hurley sticks, baseball bats and hammers. Men emerging from Holy Cross School with their children ran to join in. They were shown to the boots of the cars where they selected their weapons and joined in. The rest is of course history.

Yet even throughout the protest of 2001, not only were the causes of the problem ignored, they were made worse when the police actually insisted on using their batons to clear residents away from their own homes on Ardoyne Road, yet when their places were taken by Nationalist crowds outside Protestant homes attacking and threatening, the police did nothing. The video tapes are incredible to watch!

Now, homes in Glenbryn Park and Ardoyne Road are under attack almost every day of the week. Shots are fired but never reported by police, the INLA shoots teenagers and Sinn Fein blames Loyalists, and Republicans were not happy that local Orange Parades were dignified and peaceful, so they attacked them – twice. So, having seen the writing on the wall for years, having pleaded with the authorities to put a stop to the torture, having seen the Government dance to a Republican tune, having lost countless residents to blatant sectarian intimidation with no attempt to prevent it, and having seen another murder of an innocent man when that life could have been saved, did the people of Glenbryn really have anything about which to protest? Of course they did!

Some say street protests are dangerous and should be avoided, except as a last resort. I couldn't agree more. And in the case of Upper Ardoyne, when a population of over 3,500 has been systematically beaten and shot down to around 1,400 and all of the authorities have turned a blind eye or even assisted, then it certainly was the last resort.

Chapter Four

19th June 2001 - The straw that broke the camels back

Ardoyne, as volatile as it had ever been was about to descend back into the dark pit it had spent all those years climbing out of. What followed was a disastrous time for the Upper Ardoyne community but yet the resilience of her people united them in the fact they no longer would tolerate terrorism on their streets.

On the 19th June 2001 there was unquestionable orchestration in the concerted attack on young people putting up flags for the forthcoming July holidays (when the Protestant community celebrate their culture in the way their forefathers had always done).

A car with four Republican, burley men drove up the Ardoyne Road and drove their car towards the two young men, who were knocked off the ladders and tried to defend themselves. The men drove to Holy Cross School and turned their car to drive back into Ardoyne. Within 5 - 10 minutes approximately 30 cars came up the road full of adult men, at this point both Holy Cross and the neighbouring Wheatfield primary schools were letting the children out. The men proceeded to attack the two young men again with baseball bats from the boot of their cars and parents from Holy Cross School abandoned their children, unable to resist the temptation to join in the hand to hand fighting that had engulfed the Ardoyne Road. As the violence spread to attacks on homes, the residents of Upper Ardoyne ran to protect their property.

Protestant mothers speak of taking the hands of many of the bewildered young girls from Holy Cross and taking them back into the school grounds for safety as they had been left to observe the full fiery conflict.
Despite the frantic calls from Ardoyne Road residents, the battle intensified as no police assistance arrived. Frightened parents and children from both schools and residents of the area screaming with fear were entangled in the unruly mob. The vicious conflict raged into the night and when police came in, they did so in a heavy-handed way, beating everything in sight indiscriminately, even if they were making an attempt to calm the situation and remove the aggressors. This led to a stand-off on the Ardoyne Interface on the days that followed despite attempts by Protestant Residents to engage

with people from Lower Ardoyne to reach an appropriate resolution.

On 20th June 2001, a group of Nationalist men from Lower Ardoyne hijacked a bus carrying Protestant Schoolchildren along the Nationalist part of the road. They stood around the bus, one got on and told the hysterical children, "You are going F**king nowhere." Upper Ardoyne People were incensed, even more so because the police sat and watched the incident. They only rescued the schoolchildren when Protestant residents said, "If you don't go down – WE WILL!" Press Statements by Protestant Community to highlight their attempts to resolve the conflict

20 June 2001 - CRUA press statement

We first and foremost reject the allegation that schoolchildren have this week or at any time been prevented from making their way to or from schools in this area. The events of the past few days have followed a number of serious attacks by Nationalists on people in the Upper Ardoyne area. This is the issue. Representatives of both the Nationalist community and the minority Protestant community met to attempt to achieve a resolution to the situation, however during and after the negotiations, Protestant homes in both upper Ardoyne and nearby Twaddell Avenue were being attacked. It is clear that the conditions, under which an accommodation could be reached, do not yet exist.

In order that the prospect of a resolution can become a reality, we require an immediate end to the Nationalist siege under which the minority Protestant community finds itself at present. An immediate end to attacks by Nationalists on Protestant families both in their own streets and travelling through Ardoyne must also come to an end. Only when the siege of the Protestant Community has been lifted and intimidation brought to an end, will the conditions exist under which serious attempts can be made to achieve a resolution.

22 June 2001 - CRUA press statement

In light of the events of recent days, a public meeting was held this evening in order to initiate movement towards a resolution of the Ardoyne Road interface issue. As a result of this meeting, our community's proposal to the representatives of the Nationalist community is as follows:-

For the remaining 5 days of the school term, parents agree to continue to use the Crumlin Road entrance to and from Holy Cross School.
Both communities will issue public statements calling for an immediate end to all street protests and violence.

A Community Forum, with agreed facilitators/mediators, will be established with a view to reaching a resolution before the next school term.

Each community will put forward agreed community representatives to the forum. This will be an intensive, community-led initiative, and political representatives will not be involved.

These proposals have already been relayed to a representative of the Nationalist community. We would appeal to the Nationalist community to accept this opportunity to bring the current problems to an immediate end, and to create the space required to reach a workable resolution.

26 June 2001 - CRUA press statement

On receipt of the 'Right to Education Committee' statement of 25 June 2001, CRUA met immediately to discuss how progress could be achieved. Our response is as follows:

BEYOND THE RED GAUNTLET

1. Summary statement to be used in its entirety

"Concerned Residents of Upper Ardoyne recognise that the Ardoyne Road interface problems are the product of persistent sectarian tensions, and this is the issue that needs to be resolved. The committee of Nationalists with whom we met on 24th June 2001 has totally rejected our proposal to recognise and deal with this fundamental issue, and they should now put forward representatives who will not refuse to work with us to address ALL of our concerns. We look forward to hearing from them in this regard."

2. Full statement

"Concerned residents of Upper Ardoyne recognises that the Ardoyne Interface problems are the product of persistent sectarian tensions, and on 22nd June 2001 put forward a constructive proposal to diffuse tension and address all aspects of the sectarian problem. All citizens have the right to live free from the fear of sectarian harassment, and it is the abuse of this right by those who have attacked and intimidated Upper Ardoyne families which has led to the situation on the Ardoyne Road.

Concerned Residents of Upper Ardoyne took the initiative to seek a resolution of the issue and all symptoms of sectarianism, and it is, to say the least, disappointing that the committee of Nationalist residents in their statement of 25th June 2001 completely rejects our proposal to address the rights of all. The Nationalist Committee with which we met on 24th June 2001 is clearly not prepared to deal seriously with ALL the issues of sectarianism from which we are all suffering. In order to address this fundamental issue with the seriousness it deserves, the Nationalist committee should now put forward representatives who are prepared to address ALL of the concerns, and we look forward to hearing from them on this regard."

26 June 2001- CRUA press statement
– Following A Public Meeting of all residents in Upper Ardoyne

At 6.30pm this evening, the above-named group organised a public meeting to discuss a letter received from representatives of the Nationalist community, in relation to interface problems around the Ardoyne area. The meeting was again packed to capacity, and the response was as follows:

"In relation to the recent events at the Ardoyne Road interface, we initiated on 22 June 2001 a process which we believed would lead to swift diffusion of tensions, and to cross-community agreement to ensure that wounds were given time to heal, and anger given space to subside. As only a few days of the school term remained, we felt that this would be reasonably achievable. Our commitment to resolution was demonstrated when our community, even though still angry about repeated sectarian attacks on them, opted for compromise and dialogue. They recognised that a solution would not happen overnight, and that forcing the issues whilst tensions and anger remained could only jeopardise the prospect of an agreed resolution. Our Nationalist neighbours acknowledged this at both meetings on 20th and 24th June 2001. We are bitterly disappointed that the Nationalist representatives with whom we met have taken the decision not to allow the necessary healing space, and that they consciously jeopardised the prospect of a permanent resolution by seeking to force the issue daily, whilst tensions remained."

In their statement which refuses to deal with any issue other than that of the schoolchildren, the Nationalist representatives completely disregard the grievances and hurt of their Protestant neighbours as the result of sustained intimidation and sectarian attacks on both the Upper Ardoyne and Woodvale communities. This has contributed absolutely nothing to the prospect of resolution. To the contrary, it has had a negative impact.

*"<u>We have had no proposals from the Nationalist representatives recognising the Rights of both communities, rather than only one of them.</u> Whilst we remain eager to see a resolution as soon as possible, the matter will not be resolved until the Nationalist representatives find the courage to acknowledge that sectarianism has caused this problem, and therefore cannot be excluded from the agenda if a realistic solution is to be found. It is imperative that the Nationalist community enters into genuine dialogue with us, and we look forward to an indication that they are willing to deal with **all** aspects of this problem, and not just the element which matters to them. Our door remains open."*

The above statements outline the commitment of the community leaders in Upper Ardoyne and Woodvale to address the immediate situation that this community had found itself in. The ongoing wrangling that followed continued throughout the summer of 2001 and proved that there were elements that did not want to genuinely engage to find a resolution to the Ardoyne Road Dispute.

Following these strenuous attempts, the Upper Ardoyne Community engaged Mediation Network for NI, so that trained mediators could engage with both communities and bring a resolution to the dispute. But these meetings got off to a bad start as the community leaders from Ardoyne initially refused to engage with Mediation Network right up until 8th August. This put serious pressure on mediators to try to find an accommodation before September. (Just for reference both mediators were catholic, proving the residents of Upper Ardoyne were not out to be intolerant to another religion)

People in Upper Ardoyne truly believe that it is only a matter of time before their streets and homes will be taken over by Catholic Ardoyne and they will be evicted by whatever means it takes. They have endured poor housing and lack of amenities for many years – a coordinated attempt to remove them, that did not work; now it was back to what Nationalists do best to achieve their goal – heavy handed intimidation and attacks. It is clearly obvious that the frustration and feeling of despair within the Protestant community led to last-stand decisions to highlight their need for safety and security.

Chapter 5

The Ardoyne Road dispute - A dormant community becomes proactive

Reconciliation happens as persons or groups begin to shape their lives in positive relation to one another. It happens as people learn to deal with what separates them and as they find a bridge to new attitudes and practices that enable people to live in relation to one another, not in isolation from each other.

At the end of June 2001 the newly formed Concerned Residents of Upper Ardoyne (CRUA) requested help with cross-community talks and the "Mediation Network" was called in to help mediate between both sides of the dispute. CRUA and the people of Upper Ardoyne believed they had a breathing space which could be used to help resolve the dispute over the 10 weeks of the summer holiday. Indeed some work was carried out between the two communities, however, the mediators were instructed to let us know that the Lower Ardoyne community did not want to meet during the month of July, because of Drumcree - a road over 40 miles from the Ardoyne Road and of no significance to the talks in Upper Ardoyne. Consequently, there were no talks until 8th August 2001, 6 good weeks lost to obstinacy on the part of those in lower Ardoyne.

In early July 2001, Mr Ronnie Flanagan, Chief Constable of the RUC was cornered by the media and was asked what he was going to do regarding the children of Holy Cross and how they would get to school in September. Instead of giving a response that assisted the calls for community dialogue, he promised that he would ensure that a passage would be created along the Ardoyne Road regardless, and many believe this gave Republicans the stick with which to beat the Upper Ardoyne community over the following months. Now they did not have to engage in the mediation process to solve the dispute, they had been given a public guarantee and pathetically would use the cover of their own young children for publicity and their ongoing cry of victimhood.

Members of the Upper Ardoyne community came together one Saturday in August for training on Human Rights legislation for two reasons. One was to ensure they were having their own Human Rights protected, and secondly to ensure that they observed their responsibility of not encroaching on the Human Rights of others. This was a big step to many who had not attended a training event since school.

In August when the mediation process was kick started again it was a matter of ongoing wrangling that caused CRUA to call into question the integrity of the mediation process and indeed the veracity of the Lower Ardoyne "Right to Education Group", so the process ended.

The Northern Ireland Office intervened at the final hour and said that there was a significant group of community workers and parents who would act on behalf of the Lower Ardoyne Community and CRUA were guaranteed these people could fully represent all views in that area. A meeting was organised by the NIO who reassured CRUA of full participation by the Ardoyne group - the meeting was to be held in Belfast Castle on 31st August 2001 and all but one of CRUA's member's attended (12) but only 3 people appeared on behalf of Lower Ardoyne.

After frank discussion between both parties for almost 2 hours the members representing Lower Ardoyne told the whole group that they were not there to represent the school or any parents' views, and in fact had nothing to do with the school and that none of them have any children at the school. When asked who had asked them to attend they said it was the "Right to Education Group", but none of them attended and they said they didn't know why. CRUA members were disgusted that once again they had invested the time and effort into trying to resolve the conflict before 3rd September 2001 but to no avail, which they felt was down to gamesmanship and a lack of commitment by all those that had the power to engage and work towards a resolution. Nonetheless, they thanked the representatives from Lower Ardoyne for attending and asked them to seek out a group that could meet before 2nd September before a public meeting. On leaving the Belfast Castle those attending were informed that there was a suspect device at the gates of the Castle and the security forces had been called to investigate – obviously someone did not want the talks to go ahead. After waiting all weekend for a response from the lower Ardoyne community, CRUA could do nothing else but to call a public meeting on 2nd September 2002, as they had always adhered to the principle that decisions could only be made by the local community. The community were angry and frustrated that they had trusted the government, police, and the community workers in Ardoyne, they said, "We have no option but to hold a protest against the intimidation this community is living through. We have to let this society know what is happening to us and what we have to live with every single day". Indeed this became a motto within the community, that "Every Single Day" they would be there until their concerns were addressed.

CRUA Press Statement following Public Meeting 2nd Sept 01

03 September 2001

On 19th June 2001, Protestant and Catholic schoolchildren and parents, from Holy Cross and Wheatfield Primary schools, shared this Road. When a Republican mob stormed in and launched yet another brutal attack on Protestant residents, with no regard for the welfare of any child on the road at the time, whether Protestant or Catholic, the last shred of community relations on this Ardoyne interface was torn to pieces. Sadly, the instinct of many of the parents from Holy Cross school was not for the well-being of their children, but instead they abandoned their children on the road and forced them to witness a display of sheer genocidal hatred against the minority Protestant community here. It was Protestant mothers who rescued the children back to the safety of their own schools.

Republicans have attacked homes, taken hostage Protestant schoolchildren on a bus, prevented disabled children from accessing their school in the local Everton Centre, prevented Protestant pensioners from collecting pensions in Ardoyne, and have made the local playpark and library complete no-go areas for Protestant children. The children of the Upper Ardoyne community, the mothers, the fathers, the grandparents, have all lived in constant dread of the day when those same hate-filled faces will again be marching towards them along this road. Throughout years of sectarian harassment, the minority Protestant community here has tolerated physical attack, has tolerated intimidation and has tolerated the degrading treatment handed out to them day and daily. The Upper Ardoyne community has sacrificed security, pride, dignity, esteem, and even basic Human Rights in the interests of ALL the children - and now they are saying: ''We have nothing left to give.'' It is now almost 11 weeks since Concerned Residents of Upper Ardoyne called for a meaningful process to be set up to resolve this situation. 11 weeks in which this community has been attacked from every angle, during which Republicans orchestrated the riots which hospitalised 113 police officers, and even yesterday, Protestant pensioners were picking up the pieces of their shattered windows. What contributions have these Republicans made towards rebuilding the shattered relationship with Upper Ardoyne? And the key question - why, for 11 weeks, did representatives of the Republican community in Ardoyne refuse to engage in any process until the very last day of the holidays - this question must be answered.

The Upper Ardoyne Community has lost all trust in the ability of Republicans to control their instincts of genocidal hatred for anything Protestant. Until that relationship of trust has been rebuilt, the Upper Ardoyne community will continue its stand for the same basic Human Rights Republicans take for granted. We await from Republicans and Nationalists proposals of substance which will begin to rebuild that trust.

Chapter Six

3rd September 2002 - The mindless decision which prevented dialogue

"Through 30 years of bombs, bullets, murders and intimidation, the Upper Ardoyne community has never sought to prevent access to Holy Cross School, and still does not seek to do so. Day after day, year after year of provocation, harassment, intimidation and actual assaults by Republicans against Protestant residents have met with restraint from the Upper Ardoyne community; however the latest chain of attacks resulted in the community quite rightly taking a stand in defence of their Human Rights."

So, an ill-considered statement from the RUC's most senior officer led the Upper Ardoyne people back onto the road, where the needs of the people of Upper Ardoyne were being literally trampled on and mistreated. Were there calls from those who knew the time and effort spent by the members of CRUA, sometimes into the dead of night to find a solution – NO even those genuine concerted efforts were ignored. A community who had started with nothing but gave their all!

Police and other security forces moved into the area early in the morning of the 3rd September 2001, the residents prepared themselves to protest as they seen this was their only way to highlight the sectarian attacks on their community via the gateway of Ardoyne Road. People had had enough, they were disillusioned with the fruitless summer months and the various unproductive attempts to allow dialogue and community safety measures. They felt isolated and alone, stereotyped as child abusers they had nothing to lose only their own integrity, which they were not ready to give up so easily. As one resident said, "Nationalists treat the Protestant people here like doormats- they wipe their feet on us on the way in, and again on the way out." Gradually people emerged from the silent streets not knowing what to expect but knowing something had to be done to expose to the world that they were suffering and they had tried to resolve the issues without protest. With little community infrastructure and no knowledge of media and propaganda and certainly not knowing what was ahead of them the residents came to stand in defiance of how they had been treated and how they wanted safety for their children.

Residents knew that people might see them as sectarian, bigoted scum. The truth of the matter was however, they were frustrated that their community was consistently ignored, their issues and concerns were brushed under the carpet and they believed they had received no justice. Maybe it was time for those who had recklessly condemned the people of Upper Ardoyne to consider why a beleaguered community decided to take such a step after so long doing nothing. You can't kick a community in the teeth for thirty years and not expect them to eventually bite your foot. There are no tears for our children, no swarms of media highlighting our problems, no wails of "scum" when our pensioners are scared half to death by nationalist mobs, no condemnation when our community is battered with Hurley bats.

As people gathered to make a stand, under siege of masses of security forces and their armoured vehicles and as they tried to erect Perspex fencing to hem the community into the streets of Hesketh Road and Park. The apprehension and fear was palpable and there was disbelief of the sight that lay before them and how the British Government, NI Executive and NIO had sent them as lambs to the slaughter to appease a numerically superior aggressor. A statement was read out to the RUC, residents, and media of how this community was left with no alternative but to peacefully protest at the gateway of their attacks – On the Ardoyne Road. Residents gathered on both sides of the pavement and in the middle of the road to implement their justified right to peacefully protest against sectarian intimidation and in defence of their Human Rights. They had been told, Stay on the pavement or on the white line in the middle of the road and you are protesting peacefully."

The RUC read out the Public Order Act and sent a swarm of black bodies with batons to the ready, towards the unarmed residents, many of whom were senior citizens who had lived through eradication of Protestants from

Lower Ardoyne many years before. Many had also served in the security forces to build a better country free from intimidation, and now were confronted by several hundred RUC officers who became better known as 'Ninja's' due to their aggressive dress, acting on behalf of the crown under which many residents had served so loyally, repelling those so well known Republican faces who have tried to murder them.

The rows of black uniforms started to stomp their feet, they charged towards the defenceless crowd beating them with batons, many had their backs to them but were beaten from behind and kicked from under RUC shields. A blind man was kicked and beaten by the legal war machine before being plucked from the crowd and beaten behind the lines of RUC. There were shouts to stop, and people yelled "this man is blind" but in a flash he was gone, the swarm of black vicious strangers opened their ranks, dragged him along the ground on his behind and as though nothing had happened reformed to make their wall of fear and choose their next innocent victim. People were beaten, women and children going to the nearby Wheatfield School were entangled in the ruthless attack on this community – there was no right to education for these children, no thought for the men and women who had served their country in the past and only wanted to live in peace. This aggression launched by the RUC turned a peaceful protest into a devastating day of conflict – which was flashed around the world. Most definitely a day the Government, NI Assembly and NIO played straight into the hands of the SF/IRA and pushed Protestants further 'into the cold' by contributing to their propaganda.

The residents and Protestant schoolchildren were pushed towards the Holy Cross School and the few houses that preceded it. The RUC and Army relentlessly lashed out and attacked those within reaching distance, many ran for their lives but were beaten into gardens and told to stay there or they would be beaten further and arrested. Garden fences of Protestant homes were torn from their foundations, one group of residents held up a length of fencing to protect themselves from the barrage of batons and the onslaught from RUC officers. A pregnant woman was beaten to the ground and suffered a broken arm and as her husband tried to come to her aid he was snatched away and beaten as well. An ambulance was called to take the pregnant girl to hospital for treatment. A senior citizen stood with his legs from the knees down black from sly underhanded kicks from the officers steel toe capped boots.

Known Republican henchmen including the Shankill bomber gathered at the interface and gradually made their way towards the Ardoyne road under the cover of young Catholic girls as young as four. In fact at one point captured on video a burley crowd of approx. 50 muscle-men with no children marched their way up the Ardoyne Road, military-style towards the Holy Cross School – we have to ask questions of why was this allowed; Was this not a risk of a public order situation; or were the Protestants the lesser of two evils that day and someone to blame in a situation they did not know how to handle!

Then came the procession of Republican persecutors who used young children as pawns in this bloody conflict. Yet the same security forces whom they said they couldn't trust, including the RUC, now formed a guard of honour for them along the Ardoyne Road, with a heavily flanked path to grant their unhindered journey.

Yes, the residents and people of the area were angry and went ballistic, losing control shouting and screaming at those who paraded in front of them, especially when terrorists like the Shankill bomber – who murdered mother's, grandparents and young children, jubilantly marched past shouting "you need another fish shop"- referring to the shop he bombed. Many walked and shouted abuse but behind the view of the world's media.

Immediately, the children were taken home in a fleet of black taxis that had been hidden and waiting at the back entrance of the school from early morning, proving some say that the whole morning was nothing but a publicity stunt and a political point scoring exercise to cover up more sinister events around the world.

September 3, 2001 Posted: 6:36 PM EDT – CNN.com - The governors of a Belfast Catholic primary school are urging parents to take their children by an alternative route after violence plagued the start of the new term. The governors said they would be recommending that the children use the back entrance to the school, avoiding the loyalist Glenbryn area.

On Monday the chairman of the school's board of governors, Father Aidan Troy, announced *it's the board's recommendation that children should temporarily use an alternative entrance through the grounds of an adjacent school until the dispute was resolved.*
Julie Hyland- 5th September 2001 – WSWS.org

Belfast Lord Mayor Jim Rodgers condemned the police handling of the situation. He said: *"I have been abused this morning by some police officers and I think my position as first citizen of Belfast has been badly let down."*

The following day, the same scenes occurred with the security forces giving no thought to "the right to life" for the residents and children who lived in Upper Ardoyne. Residents were now living under siege 'twenty four seven', many were callously beaten including senior citizens and children, residents felt frustrated and showed indignation to the RUC especially as they had terrorized them in front of the world. The condemnations started to pour in from those who knew nothing of the real situation and could they not comprehend that people had not just jumped up one morning and decide to protest near a school. Had they all of a sudden become sectarian towards these schoolchildren, who as the Principal of Holy Cross said herself "had not been touched over the past 32 years of the schools life there"?

Elsewhere in North Belfast, on the 4th September a 16 year old Protestant schoolboy was knocked off his bike and killed in a hit and run incident. It was widely believed that there was a sectarian motive behind the crime although at the time of writing the court case is still pending. Three people were arrested one of which was charged with murder. A convoy of 12 cars full of residents went to visit the place where the young boy had died and laid flowers as a tribute to his young life. Many residents were very angry that day as the media crawled all over the Ardoyne Road for a meaningless photo of someone shouting that they could hype up while a child lay dead but there was no or very little media coverage on what had happened to him. Again the media got their priorities right – it did not matter about truth, the over exaggerated media hype was more important than any truth – that's what sold newspapers.

To the further detriment of the Upper Ardoyne community and their plight, there was a blast bomb thrown at RUC police lines on 5th September 2001, no-one could have known about this accept those that had planned it. Yet the police confronted and gave chase to a group of young people who were now part of an ever growing crowd. 4 RUC Officers were injured, and this happened at the same time as the children from Holy Cross were being escorted up the Ardoyne Road. Some Upper Ardoyne Community Representatives and Public representatives publicly wept and were distraught at what had just happened.

The whole environment turned a lot more menacing, landrover's and security vehicles arrived onto the Ardoyne Road on mass and engaged in a concerted attack on all the residents down the adjoining side streets. The members of the RUC embarked on a vicious assault, sweeping through resident's homes beating a 15 year old boy who was in his grandmother's home, in another a mother with a very young child were thrown to the side as the RUC crashed through the front door of their home where they unleashed a savage onslaught and wrecked most of the contents therein. "Not even an apology when they realised there was only me and the baby here" said the woman "We hadn't even been out of the house, how will I ever sleep in this house again" she cried, all because my young son in law and his friend were standing outside my house as they were trying to leave to bring home my new little granddaughter from hospital. This woman had to have hospital treatment due to the trauma of that day and is still affected today. The command to unleash rabid officers was a poignant one, as legal terror swamped through the streets of Glenbryn and on into Alliance, they growled and snarled at anyone who dared to look or speak to them. The heavy hand of the RUC officers, many who did not know the area, never mind the people, wailed their batons at anyone who came in their path. Remembering this was approx. 10.00am, children were going to school, residents were going to work and parents were already upset at their children being kept from school due to the security forces blocking the streets, all of these certainly were a breach of people's human rights. Whatever happened to the principle of "presumed innocent until you are proven guilty?" which is outlined in the Human Rights Act 1998? Since when has membership of or association to a 'community' become a crime? Law enforcement of the sort practiced in Upper Ardoyne is more indicative of a police territory than a democracy that values human rights safeguards of:

Article 2	Right to Life
Article 3	Prohibition of Torture
Article 5	Right to Liberty and Security
Article 6	Right to A Fair Trial
Article 8	Right to Respect for Private and Family Life
Article 9	Freedom of conscious, thought and religion
Article 10	Freedom of Expression
Article 11	Freedom of Assembly and Association

Later on the evening of 5th September 2002, a public meeting was called to address the ensuing violence that had crept into the legitimate right to peacefully protest, people were angry at how they had been treated by Republicans, RUC and Government. Community leaders called for calm and a decision on whether the protest should continue due to the previous events. There was an overwhelmingly loud response of YES! "We need to have our safety, tell them to build a wall across the road and shut us in, we can't use the shops, our senior citizens have been subjected to attacks attending the post office and our children are being harassed and attacked every other day on buses to and from school – Shut us in and we can build our own little community;" Was the immediate response from the floor; So the protest was to continue!

From that day on the protest undertook many changes, at public meetings people put forward ideas to disentangle the children from the loop in which they had been intertwined by those with another agenda, an agenda that was believed to be a cover for other events throughout the world, including Columbia and the arrest of 3 known Republicans who it was believed had engaged in terrorist activity. To highlight this, the residents of Upper Ardoyne held a Columbian day where they dressed up in sombreros and ponchos and held posters of those arrested. Residents started to hold theme days to highlight their plight, for example they held a victims day with all the details of the people in the area who had been murdered by Republicans throughout the years. There was a human rights day where they held posters highlighting each of their rights being denied and there was a children's day where activities, barbeques, bouncy castle etc., was organised to lift the spirits of the children living within the Upper Ardoyne area. This proved an excellent morale builder for the residents as well who felt positive about organising it and uniting the various sections of the Upper Ardoyne Community.

I must mention 3 women from outside of the community who attended the protest every single day, they used to come with all different things to cheer the community up so they came with masks, jokes, funny stories and everyone got to know them as the "Flying Pickets." I must say the community would want me to commend these girls for their dedication in coming everyday to lighten the heavy hearts of all those who stood for their right to live in safety. All 3 of you added to the experience and your commitment to the community will be remembered.

The protest itself changed as days went on, residents realised that they had to take the children out of the complex equation but they were not going to do this to the detriment of their protest. They knew their protest was not against children it was against terrorists who wanted the world to believe it was against the children. The residents decided to use whistles and horns as residents were finding it really difficult not to shout at the well known Republicans walking up the road. This changed after a few days to incorporate silent protests when the children went up with their parents and only blew whistles and horns when the parents and Republicans came back down. The children from Holy Cross sang as they came home from school each day with "Everywhere we go, people always ask us who we are" and Hey Baby, I want to know if you'll be my girl." A site rarely shown by media!

One of the day's of the first week, local gospel singers came to sing Christian songs in the middle of the road, probably their way of sending a message to the people protesting and in all probability to those walking up the road. Almost certainly responding to a complicated situation in the only way they could at that moment in time– the RUC also persisted in pushing and grappling with these church men to push them off the road before the parents would appear.

On 7th September the protest was postponed in respect of the funeral of the young 16 year old, Thomas MacDonald, killed earlier in the week. CRUA asked the parents to use an alternative route on this day to give space for a memorial service for the young boy on the Ardoyne Road but this was denied and parents insisted that the "School run" go ahead that day as usual. Rev Hamilton and Father Troy said a prayer together outside Holy Cross

School. A large number of residents represented Upper Ardoyne at he young lad's funeral. - Press Release from CRUA regarding suspension of protest

Protest Suspended as Mark of Respect - 12 September 2001
As a mark of respect to the thousands of innocent victims of Tuesday's terrorist attacks on the United States, the Ardoyne Road protest against the intimidation of the Upper Ardoyne community will be suspended for Friday 14th September 2001. Our sincerest sympathy goes to the families and friends of all of those who have suffered the loss of loved ones, and we trust that the Nation will unite in opposition to those who seek to weaken it through acts of terrorism.

The Upper Ardoyne community has also suffered loss of life at the hands of terrorism, and a short memorial service had been planned in advance, for Ardoyne Road, Thursday 13th September at 8.30am. In light of this week's atrocities, it is proper that this service should still proceed, when we will unite in grief with the people of the United States. The suspension of the protest for the above-named reasons was agreed at a public meeting on Wednesday evening, 12th September.

13th September 2001 - A memorial service was held in respect for all those who had lost their lives in the USA to terrorism. 14th September 2001 - Residents felt that they had been the victims of terrorism for years and that they must cancel the protest that day – one resident remarked "after all that is what our protest was all about, the acts of terrorism against this community is no longer acceptable".

A member of the committee contacted the Police Ombudsman, to ask her to come to the Ardoyne Road to witness what was happening with regards to police heavy-handedness, and requested her help to ensure things were done properly but she said she could not attend as that would compromise her impartial position. Yet a while later she did visit the Ardoyne Road and stood a couple of hundred yards away from Holy Cross School, after which she made a public condemnation of the protestors. Was this her role there! So much for impartiality! and it certainly brings into play the reasons why every single complaint that has been submitted to the Police Ombudsman's office from the Upper Ardoyne area relating to police brutality and attitude during the weeks of the protest have been turned down unequivocally even if there were witnesses. Could everybody have been wrong!

On 19th September arrests were made against the Upper Ardoyne Community which many people of the area believe was a campaign to discredit the committee they had elected. Throughout the summer months this committee had done nothing other than to try and have a positive impact on ongoing events and engage with the Catholic community which was witnessed by NIO and others. A lot of the trumped-up charges were dropped after the protest ended when the evidence could not support the allegations and out of date laws that were used. This only fuelled the fire with local people; was there was a method in their madness i.e. arrest and charge members of their committee and it will kick them in the teeth further and teach them not to stand up again for their rights; but it did not happen like that, things had gone too far and residents felt for once in their lives that they were doing something for their community and future, "at least now people are starting to listen," said an elderly protestor "they all hate us but they are listening".

CRUA "suspended all business until further notice" due to the arrest of some of its members.

Court bars six from Ardoyne school protests
A court has banned six men from taking part in loyalist protests at a North Belfast girls' primary school.

Belfast Magistrates Court ordered the men to stay away from the protests and the Holy Cross School in Ardoyne.

All six were charged with unlawfully fighting and making an affray on September 3.

That was the day the protests resumed when the children returned to school after the summer holidays.

All six were remanded on bail of £400 until November 15

Story filed: 13:25 Thursday 20th September 2001
– excerpt from Ananova

The crowds going up and down the road were swelling and it became a joke with residents that the kids going to the school must have had 3 or 4 parents each. There were so many and even at one point journalists started to say "what is going on here, there's three times as many adults as children"! Some of those going up and down the road were teenage schoolchildren themselves also a one-liner by now - that he/she had her child young. Many made comments on the amount of men going up and down the road and the media started to ask questions, because they knew who many of them were.

This community that had little to no community infrastructure started to see the protest as a way to engage with each other, they became very united and supportive of their collective task of highlighting their serious security and safety concerns. As well as this it became a time when residents could meet, interact and talk about the issues that affected their everyday life. The unification of the community at the protest filled the vacuum that had been created throughout the years of conflict and fears of danger; after all they could stand and talk in the street and had a huge security presence to protect them. Although many condemned the actions of this small community, the positive effects of togetherness and the long overdue social interaction contributed to the feeling of recovery, wellbeing and a sense of warmth and personal support.

A local mother, stood at the local bus-stop waiting for transport to go to work, a female parent who walked the school route everyday pulled up in a car with another woman and ensure a ferocious attack on the girl, trailing her by the hair along the pavement while her other assailant kicked and punched her. They escaped by their car leaving the young mother lying injured and comatose by the roadside until passers-by ran to get medical assistance.

Day by day relationships built up between residents, considering most of the people who came out to protest were senior citizens, many had not spent time with each other for years. Old friendships reignited and everyday was like a coffee morning, people started to arrive earlier so they could have more time with their friends. Some actually started to plan funny things to do so they could make everybody laugh. But as time went on people got tired and felt the strain of the constant condemnation bandwagon.

Ongoing throughout the protest public meetings were held to always have the mandate of the local people and what they wanted to do. Brice Dickson from the Human Rights Commission visited the Ardoyne Road to see what was going on and commented that what he had seen that day was a legal protest. Members of the committee had spoken to Brice and asked him for his advice on whether he thought using buses would be a good idea, the committee felt at this time that an idea to keep both sets of children safe and take them out of the equation would be to get the parents and children from Holy Cross to use buses provided by BELB. BELB agreed to the use of these and CRUA released a statement saying that the community were putting this forward as an idea to get around the impasse and start to build a breathing space for dialogue. But this was turned down immediately as parents said they would be frightened of their children on the buses in case they were attacked. A suggestion was made that a member of the committee could travel on each bus but again this was rejected.

Many people made sweeping judgements about **all** the people that lived in Upper Ardoyne and instead of looking beyond the shields, the riots, the protest, to find the residents of Upper Ardoyne, the people who had accepted and participated in cross community activities for their children and the children from Holy Cross; People who had Irish dancing in their local community centre for both communities to take part in for over a year and a half with no hassle; who only wanted to live in peace.

One woman said she could not believe the depths some people went to, to exclude and degrade this community. She said, "My cat died which I had for many years, I was heartbroken as I lived on my own and he was my dearest friend. I decided I would rather give a homeless cat a home from a refuge rather than get a kitten. So I rang the cat home and explained what had happened and how long I had had my cat. The girl was very sympathetic knowing by the sound of my voice I was distressed at the loss of my old friend, and she said it was very good that I had thought of going there to get a homeless cat.

She said she needed to complete a form over the phone and explained the costs etc., attached to taking the pet, I agreed this was fine and she proceeded to complete the form with my name and address. She said she would take a minute to check something out and would come back to me in a moment. When she returned she said "I am very sorry but I am not allowed to let you have a cat from this refuge," when I asked why? She replied, "We have had a memo from our head office which states that no cats are allowed to be re-homed in your area due to the state of affairs there." I replied "I have reared my children and grandchildren here." But she said "I am sorry but I would lose my job if I allowed a cat to be re-homed in that area."

Many lies were told throughout the time of the protest and many things were exaggerated including the fallacy that balloons, filled with urine and faeces, were thrown at parents and children – "This is a downright lie" said one resident "What's wrong is there is nothing bad happening for them to hype up so now they are just making up pure unadulterated lies. There are two women coming up here everyday who are going out of their way to cause hassle they are real troublemakers."

It was always the feelings of the residents, that all that was needed to move forward was compromise on both sides of the conflict to resolve the issues and for both sides to accept and contribute to resolving each other's difficulties.

Residents felt they had on many occasions tried to come to a compromise with their counterparts but always hitting a brick wall when everything they suggested was blanked.

From 2nd to 5th November, CRUA engaged in intensive meetings with senior police to try to ease the environment for the children in the whole situation. CRUA had came up with a number of proposals including removal of riot uniforms to reflective jackets and soft hats, thinking this will ease tension and produce a more conducive environment for progress. Stuart McCartney was reported in the media saying "He welcomed the recognition by police that the protest was legitimate and we were working with the police to try to remove the children from the equation."

On the other hand the residents felt no matter how they tried, all their efforts were thrown back in their faces. Parents had complained from the first day that it had been ridiculous children had to be escorted by police in riot gear, yet a comment in the local news by one parents said, " parents and children felt vulnerable because of the reduction in security measures. I'm not happy with the scaling down." CRUA member said, "no matter what we do it has to be misconstrued." Father Troy said he welcomed the "change in Attitude, but was still worried what was going on."

The Upper Ardoyne community had always believed that their safety and that of their families was paramount, they were living in a constant state of siege and they had persisted that if there was a way to remove the children from the situation they would, their whole argument was that their children could not live safely. So when a community safety package was offered by the First and Deputy First Ministers, a public meeting was held to review it and endorse a suspension of the protest 'if it was acceptable to the local community'. The following statement was agreed.

Press Release from CRUA regarding the Suspension of "The Protest"
Protest Suspended - 24 November 2001

Protestant residents of the Glenbryn area of North Belfast last night voted to suspend their protest on Ardoyne Road 'in order to pave the way for constructive dialogue'. The decision came at 10.00 pm (24/11/01) last night when, following days of speculation, a packed community meeting voted in favour of the residents' committee's recommendation to suspend the 22 week old protest immediately. It is understood that although reservations were expressed by a small number of residents, they agreed to the suspension in order to 'give the peace plan a fair opportunity to deliver safety and the prospect of normality in the Glenbryn area.

'North Belfast DUP MP Nigel Dodds refuted the suggestion that the peace package would be seen as a reward for sectarianism. ''The measures discussed are in fact long overdue, and should be seen as deserved by the community rather than a special favour from anyone'' he said. North Belfast City Councillor and MLA Billy Hutchinson added: ''No-one should be looking for negatives in this. The protest has been suspended and what needs to happen now is for the Nationalist community to get into dialogue with the people of Glenbryn. That is what will bring about a complete solution to the dispute.'' Mark Coulter of the Concerned Residents of Upper Ardoyne added: ''Safety concerns have been raised constantly by this community over the past four or five years and have been ignored. Tonight we were able to say to the residents that their safety is now being taken seriously, that they should give these plans a chance to work, and the community accepted that.'' Mr Coulter also cautioned; ''Nationalists should recognise the fragility of the situation and react with sensitivity.''

Chapter Seven

Perceptions of an orchestrated media campaign

"Despite the best efforts of the mainstream media to portray the Ardoyne Dispute as a protest against a Catholic School, Concerned Residents of Upper Ardoyne has maintained from the 19th June 2001 that Holy Cross School has simply become entangled in a wider interface problem which has been simmering for years."

The media have often have the power to pigeon-hole some people into identities that may have negative consequences - i.e. Protestant residents being classed in the media as mere sectarian thugs and child abusers. At first people try to overcome this label but due to ongoing media campaigning they see no other way to but to act accordingly and identify with the media's negative label (*self fulfilling prophecy - social interactionists view*) However, some refuse to conform to these labels and still fight to shirk off the label no matter how detrimental the media campaign is to their reputation, in the belief that they are doing the right thing for their community. Both of these are clear stereotypes imposed on Protestant communities especially in North Belfast.

This is was particularly evident in Upper Ardoyne where due to the residents belief that Republicans used young girls from Holy Cross school to create a media extravaganza, so the real issues were hidden from the world which would only see frightened children trying to go to school, petrified by the scenes forced upon them by **all** the adults involved that day, including PSNI, Nationalists and under provocation the protestors. But known Republicans had been invading this Protestant enclave and threatening and attacking Protestant children, some of which has been documented both in written and video format.

But most of the coverage of the dispute regarding Upper Ardoyne was covered with damning, bitter misunderstanding of the issues as the following article shows:

"Last week, children in Ardoyne were prevented from going to Holy Cross primary school by loyalists who could no longer tolerate a couple of

hundred Catholic five- to eleven-year-old girls accompanied by their parents passing their front doors on the way to school." Republican News **20/06/01**

No-one wanted to stop young children going to school said one parent angrily, *"there has been no problem from the young children going to school and there was never a couple of hundred children accompanied by their parents, most used cars or the entrance at Crumlin Road. And as for 'tolerate' we have had to tolerate blatant murder in our community not to mention all the verbal abuse and attacks that don't even make the media."*

Protestant children have been regularly attacked and physically and emotionally hurt in school buses going to and from school. Men with screwdrivers have set upon young people, who were walking to school. Women going to shops have been harassed and senior citizens told not to come back to the local post office both of which are situated in the catholic area of Ardoyne. Many people have been attacked at the nearest local bus-stop, one woman to the extent she needed hospital treatment and indeed her attacker walked up the Ardoyne Road everyday following the attack and although this was highlighted - nothing happened. The media did in fact cover the story of the attack but never went into detail of attackers and detail that it was certainly sectarian and pathetically tried to justify it by asking the injured party if they were part of the ongoing protest.

The media certainly can impact on how an event is perceived. An excellent analogy of this is when a young Catholic postman was murdered, postal workers and teachers were threatened - The chairman of the Irish Congress of Trade Unions called for a massive protest to show the world that we were against sectarian intimidation, schools closed, businesses closed etc., to come out and support his call. The media promoted it as an event for peace and a word to terrorists that they were no longer welcome to threaten our society. BUT, how then did the same kind of call by those residents in Upper Ardoyne, of whom many were elderly and had suffered the threats of sectarian intimidation personally, the murder in their streets and the horrific attacks on their children by Republicans not have the same positive media coverage. Why was the story portrayed to be so negative and yet both are identical, instead the residents of the area were branded sectarian bigots, child abusers and scum of society - were they not doing just as the Chairman of the ICTU had done? Saying NO to sectarian intimidation; Yes! They were the same, but the media did not want to portray this, all they were interested in was this fantastic media story of crying little girls of Holy Cross School, a perception that was created by the media and elements of Republicanism, and flagged up all around the world for ulterior motives. No mention of the real genuine issues. This community have been asked by members of the press and media "did we not ask you for your side of the story" and they have replied " yes, but you distorted it to give your dramatised story an alleged balance but really there was no investigative journalism at all just melodramatic reporting which assisted only further to cover up the real issues in this area.

Do I blame the journalists and those on the ground at the times of intense media attention; not all the time, I believe that there were those who wanted their great, exaggerated story but I feel there were those on the ground who saw for themselves that there was something that had caused a community after all these years to stand up and say we have had enough - but this was distorted and dramatised by editors who wanted to sell papers rather than tell the true story. The propaganda machine was set into motion says a young parent; "we didn't have a chance once the media sank their teeth into one of the biggest news stories to hit the headlines". They fell over themselves to reach a person, anyone who was a protestor or related to a protestor or their granny was a protestor! Anyone would do; they did not want the real reasons or an explanation of why residents were there; they just wanted to 'balance' the argument; truth just did not come into it.

Many Protestants believe that the media have consolidated relationships with nationalist/Republicans and even now when reports are written, whether they mean to or not they perpetuate the feeling of prejudice. i.e. If there is an incident in which Protestants are responsible the media carry the line "a pipe bomb (which probably turned out to be a fire work) was thrown at Nationalists by Protestants in Upper Ardoyne yet if there is an incident where Nationalists are involved media carry the line: "there are reports of shooting in the Ardoyne area - not declaring from where or by who. Now this I believe could be perceived as paranoia but when it happens 9 times out of every 10 maybe there are bona fide reasons why Protestants feel as they do.

Reporters and journalists make the arguments that they cannot get Protestants to engage with the them and have actually at times asked the media to leave scenes of conflict due to their mistrust of their reporting. Their argument is that on the Nationalist side they can get many people to come forward to speak to them and portray their story. Speaking to residents they understand this assertion by the media but they do feel paranoid if they go onto TV or in the newspapers as then people will unjustifiably target them in the city centre or to other public places which has happened in the past. Not only do they worry for themselves which many have said they would take a risk, but they worry in case they are with family members or friends and then they are putting them at risk also.

Many people felt that they had at times tried to contact the media to highlight positive images of North Belfast and some of the excellent work that was happening in these areas, but the media were apathetic in covering community issues, only the overdramatic, sensationalised stories hit the news headlines and certainly this was one of the biggest and best that had been created and didn't just happened overnight.

Chapter Eight

The forgotten children

Family and community life should provide children with love, caring, nurturing, bonding and the sense of identity, belonging and permanence that will best enable them to grow, develop and thrive. All children should benefit and be enriched by being part of an inclusive environment that promotes physical, social, and intellectual well-being which should lead to independence and self-determination.

The children living in Upper Ardoyne and in fact many who live in North Belfast cannot have the luxury of being part of an inclusive society where equality reigns. Areas and young people have become segregated through no fault of their own and some will argue that the educational system should promote integrated education without the complexity of religion. This is not to say that children do not deserve to have their religious education but that it should be outside of the educational environment. Many feel that if children grow up together interacting throughout their school lives and from a very young age, then they will have the option to make informed choices about those who practice a different religion, but in reality are no different to them.

Throughout the campaign of intimidation, attacks, media hype and serious concern, were a group of children who not only lived in the Upper Ardoyne area 24 hours a day but had no facilities or designated workers to work with them and their immediate emotional and physical concerns. These were the forgotten children in all of this. At no point before, during or after the protest did anyone ask about the children who live in Upper Ardoyne. How are they coping! Do they need support! Not only were they under siege in their own streets by the large security presence but they were verbally abused by those who were there to protect children from the other side of the divide.

Young people were beaten with batons as the PSNI gave chase after those who threw a blast bomb at them and did they investigate or take note of the video footage they had of that day, NO they immediately reacted and engaged in a run of terror through the streets and beat young people, ransacked homes with no-one there to resist but young babies in prams or their mothers arms – where were those children's rights and their right to education, they could not get to school until the 'School Run' as the PSNI called it was over. Indeed on the 31st October (Halloween) parents and children had waited until the streets were clear to take their children to school but a group of Catholic parents decided they wanted to come back up the road to Holy Cross to join in their child's party but they had only left to walk down the road not 20 minutes earlier, didn't they stay in the school. The powers that be that day in the disguise of a PSNI Inspector who became known as "Nasty Nick," took the irrational decision to deploy once again the 40 or so landrover's and police officers to escort the party goers back up the road. When challenged about why the area was going to be under siege again within 20 minutes of them leaving, he said it was his decision and the parents had to get back up to the school, by this time many officers had got out of their vehicles and proceeded to push and baton charge a group of approx 8 women with a child in a pram and a young 16 year old girl. What happened next was a travesty, the mother of the baby in the pram was thrown over a landrover, the child's pram was thrown to the side of the pavement where it toppled and the baby was thrown out, as the 16 year old girl went to lift the baby and the pram she was battened over the back by another officer. As another young mother tried to engage with the police and ask why this was happening a police officer ran approx. 6 feet and using his steel toed issued boot kicked the woman between the legs where she fell to the ground in agony. This happened in full view of a couple of community workers who had just driven away from the area when the security forces had pulled out the first time. When they came back on the scene a PSNI officer said" you deserve this – you voted yes!

Children in Upper Ardoyne as young as three years old were attending nursery school acting out the roles of those who fought in their streets with their parents (PSNI), when they tried to get them to school they were told to take an alternative route which they daren't ask of the children of Holy Cross for the outrage it would cause.

The children and young people of Upper Ardoyne were abused, lived through the riot situations and conflict on the Ardoyne Road, could not play at their homes on the Ardoyne Road for fear of attack or being blamed on starting another riot just because they were there, had no dedicated facility or staff to work with them and take them on trips out of the area or address the issues they had living in this volatile interface which was blasted around the world as the worst place to be – 'amongst child abusers'. Although these issues have been brought out and raised with the Government and authorities, still there is no proper intervention in this area to provide qualified, dedicated youth workers to help these young people develop and to look at the issues they have to live with everyday. OFM/DFM have through the North Belfast Action Project provided funding for interventions with young people for a 3 month period Aug – Nov 2002 but what about the long term, throwing short term money into areas with absolutely no community infrastructure or established workers has only created further pressure on the voluntary community workers in the neighbourhood.

The only support the children had was from Wheatfield Primary School and the dedicated staff, led by a principal who would not succumb to the use of children in his school as part of the extravagant media battle, even though they had threats from the 'Catholic Reaction Force' and a number of suspect bombs. He knew only too well that his children were suffering as well, if not more, than those from their neighbouring school but he sought out help behind closed doors and did not use his children as tools to respond in a way that would cause them further distress. This was a man of dignity who had pride in his school and the young children that attended it, he knew the detrimental effects of throwing young children into the media and decided to support the children and their parents in the only way he knew how – in a safe environment free from the waging war of criticism and abuse that was being launched by a school a few hundred yards from his.

Yes many times the principal of that other school told of the horrific stories of her young girls and did nothing only contribute to the negativity, hype and use of children as a means to an end. Should we not ask why? A school that has become known around the world for all the wrong reasons but received many benefits and rewards for the negative publicity the principal sought.

Many times there have been reports of attacks on Protestant schoolchildren who have been physically hurt in attacks on their school buses but is there the hype or media coverage for these, again due to the lack of dedicated, experienced youth and community workers these have not been collectively monitored and recorded to highlight statistics and the actual extent of injuries.

In January 2002 both children from the Boys and Girls Model Schools had to be taken past Ardoyne in the back of police landrover's to meet their parents waiting for them at Twaddell Avenue as there were fears for the children's safety.

Walk of Shame

◀ A community under siege - with all rights denied.

◉ A banner with a double edged message:
1. Shame that the children were used as pawns.
2. Shame that the world did not acknowledge the issues of Upper Ardoyne.

◉ Parent gives a triumphant jeer to Upper Ardoyne.

▲ Preparations for community relations.

▼ Guard of honour for one community, denial of rights for the other.

▲ Residents defence against aggression.

BEYOND THE RED GAUNTLET

The police said they were concerned about the safety of the children had they attempted to walk down the Crumlin Road.
- BBC Website – 09/01/02

If children should have safe passage to and from school (which of course they should) then why is it so unsafe for children from areas such as Shankill, Ballygomartin, Glencairn, Highfield to walk past the Ardoyne shop fronts on their way to school for many years now. Again the perception of Protestants is double standards by Nationalists who believe they have a right to walk and go wherever they please but when Protestants try to do the same they come under attack and are told this is a Catholic area. Public Representatives have to take responsibility here by guiding communities to accepting cultures other than their own instead of exacerbating the situation with comments that instil the genuine and very real perception of no-go areas. These areas need leadership, leadership that can plan for the future of our young people, care about their education, programmes that teach them tolerance, acceptance and Lifeskills to help them deal with their identity and how to deal with difficulties in their lives, empowering our young people to make better choices.

Adolescents in the Upper Ardoyne area are consistently being drawn into the conflict not through choice but it is an unavoidable reality that it is used as a recreational pastime, both sides of the 'peace line' kids with nothing better to do and often from areas away from the flash-points, congregate in order to kick off a riot; a pastime that has on many occasions proved to be extremely dangerous when live gunfire ricochets off lampposts, windows and the ground beside them.

Our children deserve better than this and the authorities have a responsibility not to leave these young adolescents without the social skills and Lifeskills they need to progress. I believe they are discriminated against where there are other areas that are taken by the hand. These young people are very responsive to positive input from adults. They are worthy of trained youth workers who they can turn to in times of need.

There is no place to go to engage with good role models or their peers, there are no youth programmes running to show them alternatives and no-one was taking responsibility for the children who were forgotten in this conflict.

▶ Residents of Upper Ardoyne under daily curfew.

▶ Resident wraps up for "Rights"

Why did they do this to us

▲ Little girl of two asks "why?".

Nationalists attack via Crumlin Road following football team defeat.

Public representative Cllr Billy Hutchinson denied access to footpath.

Resident literally under siege.

Chapter Nine

Twaddell Avenue - A sister Interface

Certainly if there is conflict at the Ardoyne Road/Alliance Avenue Interface then nine times out of ten it will spill out onto the Ardoyne Shop fronts /Twaddell Avenue Interface and vice versa. Indeed both Upper Ardoyne Community workers and the Community workers in Twaddell Avenue/Woodvale forged links and emergency contacts because of the inextricable link between the two interfaces.

Contributed by John Macvicar - Twaddell/Woodvale Residents Association.

The residents of Twaddell Avenue are approx 80% elderly and have lived in the area for many years in fact most of them have been there for decades and raised their families there. One elderly resident has kept a diary of all the incidents over the past 30 years, written up in a book

SAME OLD SAME OLD!!!!!!!
Bad trouble - windows smashed...........Petrol bomb thrown at front door 6.10am. Windows broken in 2, 4, 6 and 8 Twaddell Avenue! Also cars petrol bombed.............Police van petrol bombed at the corner, a taxi was stoned............Men banging on my front door its 12.45 a.m. They are shouting they are going to burn us out over Christmas.....

Heard it all before? Terrible isn't it all this trouble in Twaddell Avenue? The sad thing is this, the comments are an extract from a diary kept by a senior citizen who until recently lived at the top of Twaddell Avenue. Do you know what is even sadder? The comments are dated as follows: January 30th 1972, August 9 1986, March 5th 1986 and December 22nd 1989.

The diary details the level of sectarian violence since 1969 and includes the murder of army personnel escorting Protestant school children up the Crumlin Road. So all this media hype about naked sectarian violence needs to be put firmly into perspective, certainly as far as the Twaddell/Ardoyne roundabout interface is concerned.

⏶ The scene that met residents who just wanted to have their safety, instead they lost their freedo[m]

⏶ P.S.N.I. sit back as attack is launched on Upper Ardoyne residents.

Families flee ongoing attacks.

BEYOND THE RED GAUNTLET

The Twaddell Avenue estate was built in the late 1920's, it numbers about 600 homes mainly built in terraced rows with gardens front and rear. Almost 80% of the homes are owner occupied with the remaining under the control of the NIHE. Housing in the area is at a premium and it is usually the case that public housing only becomes available when someone dies. It is a very settled community with a disproportionately high level of adult residents in the 60+-age bracket. In fact of the 50 homes stretching on both sides from the top of Twaddell Avenue to the junction of Crumlin Gardens only 5 are occupied by families.

The residents of Twaddell are effectively suffering a war of attrition. There is a concerted, orchestrated and continual attempt to physically, verbally and psychologically intimidate the residents in this community; the ultimate goal of Republicans in Ardoyne is to make the homes at the top of Twaddell Avenue uninhabitable and by doing so destabilize the rest of the area. As part of the Outer Ring of Belfast Twaddell Avenue is a main arterial route with over 14,000 vehicles per day passing along it. As a North Belfast interface it is unique in that it is a live interface, there are no gates to close like Lanark Way, there are no barriers to close to stop traffic and there are no walls or fences to build higher. The interface is the human beings living in Twaddell Avenue attempting to live as normal a life as possible, going about their daily business - going shopping, collecting pensions, going to the library except June 19th 2001 put paid to that. Now the shopping is done on the Woodvale Road, the pensions are lifted at other post offices; the library books are collected at Shankill Library. Why? Because Ardoyne Republicans told them to go and not come back.

June 21st 2001 started out as any other day, we all knew that there had been some trouble on the Ardoyne Road but no one was prepared for what was about to unfold. Within minutes of trouble breaking out on the Ardoyne Road a mob of adult men arrived in Twaddell Avenue armed with Hurley bats, iron bars, car jacks, wheel braces, bricks, stones, bottles and laid into everything in front of them cars, windows, doors and people. It was definitely a case of same old same old. For many of the residents it was reminiscent of the '69 troubles. From then on it was a case of long days and even longer nights. From June 19th 2001 up until July 2002 the local residents association has recorded over 125 separate incidents, ranging from a few stones and bottles thrown to the full-scale attack mounted on the area on July 26 2001 when the mob from Ardoyne was continually replenished from the local pub and club. During all this there was still time for a little humor when after an attack during which a table from the pub was thrown at Twaddell Avenue one of the residents was heard to say "I know we are being asked to sit round a table and talk, but they didn't tell us they were going to throw it at us first!"

On top of all these attacks came the psychological threats in the post and on the phone - threats to burn the estate to the ground and to cap it all we had to deal with the lies, the damned lies and Sinn Fein statements. At every opportunity we tried to put our side of the story to the press and associated media but try as we might it appeared that there was a particular bias with some of the media, to the extent the BBC is "affectionately" referred to as the Biased Broadcasting Corporation. And then we struck it lucky on January 9th we had more trouble on the Ardoyne Road and true to form we had reports of mobs from Twaddell Avenue attacking the shop fronts. Unfortunately the Sinn Fein spokesman hadn't figured on CCTV footage

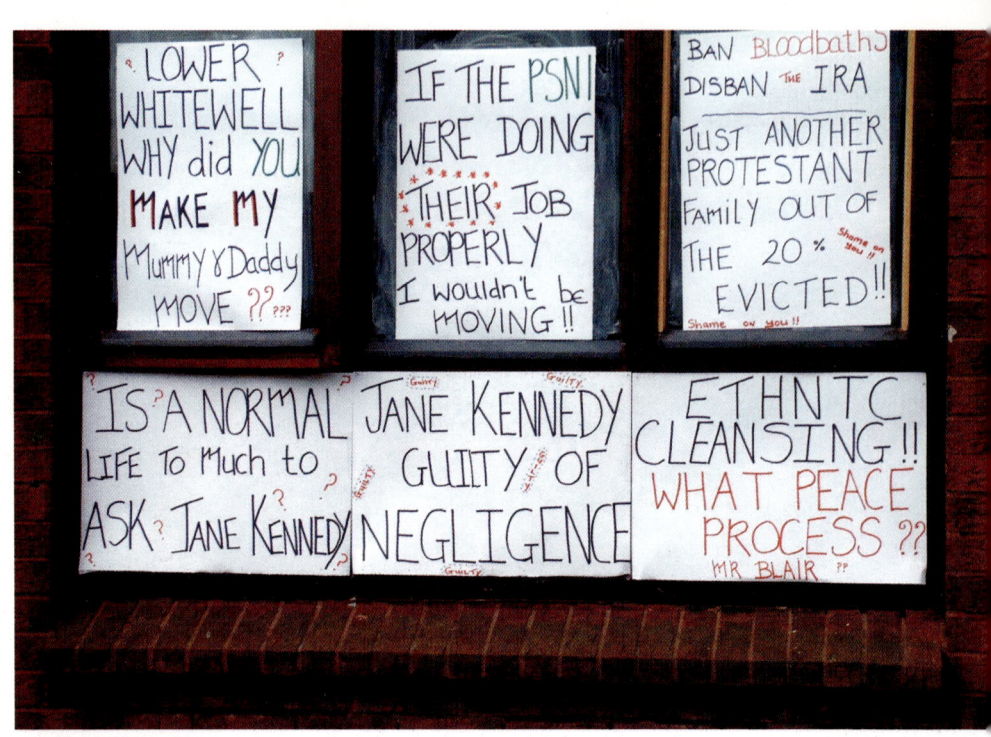

⊙ Plea's from 'White City' residents.

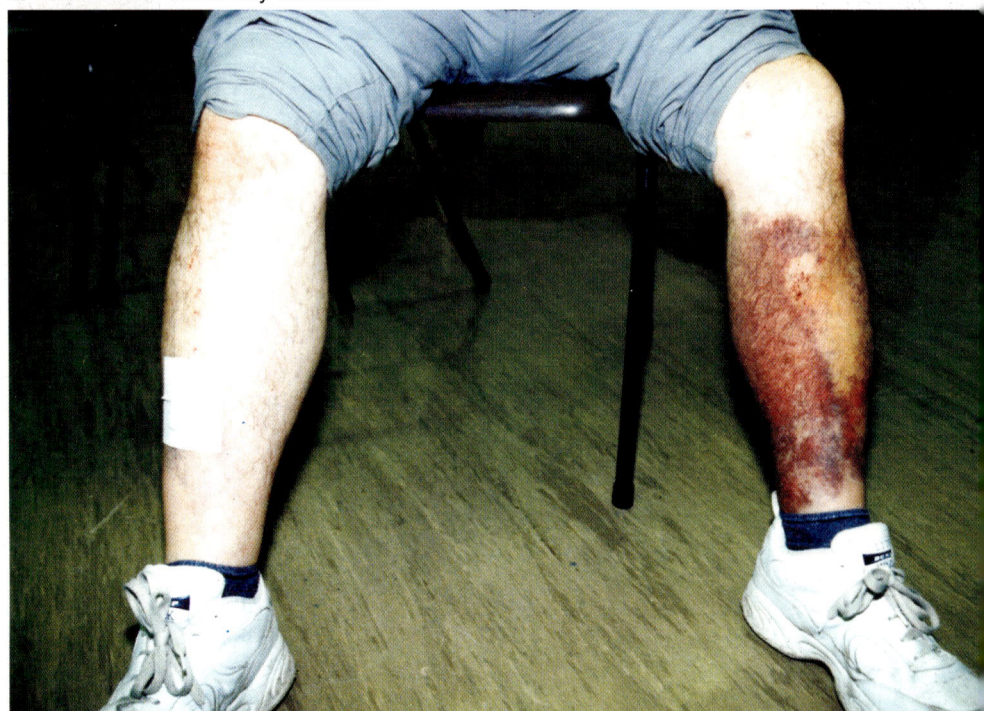

⊙ The injuries of a senior citizen, inflicted by those with the responsibility of protecting him (P.S.N

Petrol bombs thrown at protestant homes.

Police try to contain incursion into Upper Ardoyne.

that clearly showed the opposite - a crowd of Republicans attacking Twaddell from the shopfronts!!

Despite all this sectarian baggage Twaddell is a settled community, with plans to expand with the new housing development at Somerdale to include 155 new homes for sale, 35 bungalows for senior citizens, a new school to replace Forthriver Primary, an opportunity to develop a multi purpose facility to service our community and a desire to say we are here to stay.

Listening to all the Sinn Fein rhetoric over the last few months there is a feeling real or perceived, that only time will confirm, Sinn Fein/IRA are preparing to use Ardoyne and a number of other interfaces as the " new Drumcree". With regard to the attack on January 30th 1972 and all subsequent attacks, there is a simple question which remains unanswered - How many times have homes in Brompton Park been attacked by the residents of Twaddell Avenue or anywhere else for that matter since 1972?

Chapter Ten

Outcry For Community Safety - The promised package

The only demands from the Upper Ardoyne Community was that they were allowed to live in peace, without intimidation and sectarian attack - in order to help this happen measures were agreed by the Office of the First minister and Deputy First Minister Mr David Trimble and Mr Mark Durkan on 23rd November. The following is a timeline of how the lives of residents were used as a bargaining chip by the OFMDFM.

The First Minister and Deputy First Minister's initiative was announced on 23 November 2001 and the key issue was a safety package for the improvement of the Alliance Avenue interface with Ardoyne Road, which included a minor realignment of Ardoyne Road. OFM/DFM's announcement said "The target date for completion of the design is mid-January." Since then, the history reads as follows:

11 December 2001:
CRUA ask OFM/DFM for an assurance that consultation with the Nationalist community is at an advanced stage and that the project remains on target. In response, OFM/DFM says on 13 December 2001 "'Consultations are going well, and we fully intend to meet the target set in the Ministers' letter". The same message confirms that a meeting with Nationalist residents is planned "early next week". It is later confirmed that those consulted have been made aware of the principle of the scheme, and are agreeable.

11 January 2002:
An OFM/DFM representative attends a public meeting in Glenbryn at which he says that the design for the safety package including the realignment and wall, will be complete "in days or weeks, not months".

12 January 2002:
Daniel McColgan is murdered in Rathcoole. OFM/DFM subsequently reports that the Nationalist community in Ardoyne has "stepped back" from the process as a result of the murder.

13 February 2002:

CRUA registers concern that the consultation process appears to be turning into an open-ended debacle, and asks that a clear method should be adopted to prevent any further tail-chasing.

15 February 2002:

OFM/DFM reports that "Ardoyne has requested additional consultation". They also confirm that the issue of community dialogue will not be linked to the delivery of the safety package as 'a bargaining chip'. CRUA responds by querying previous assurances that consultation are going well, and with reference to the murder in Rathcoole states that whilst the Nationalist community could not be criticised for their reaction, it should have been ruled irrelevant to consultations regarding Ardoyne Road.

15 February 2002:

First Minister/DFM reports in a letter to MP Nigel Dodds (later copied to CRUA by OFM/DFM) that delays have resulted from disorder in the area in January 2002, the murder of Daniel McColgan, and threats to teachers and postal workers. They also state that "community representatives have acknowledged that there is no linkage between the establishment of a community forum and the proposed road realignment" and "if agreement cannot be reached, despite our efforts, neither community will be permitted to veto developments which we consider essential to the successful implementation of the agreed package."

19 February 2002:

OFM/DFM reports that "'Ardoyne Focus Group is now actively engaged on this consultation". AFG is an umbrella group for a substantial number of community groups in Nationalist Ardoyne.

4 March 2002:

CRUA asks OFM/DFM representative to present any design adjustments arising from consultation, for consideration.

8 March 2002:

OFM/DFM reports that Ardoyne Focus Group met with the engineers/architects responsible for the barrier/wall aspect of the safety package design brief. The report states "Consultations with Ardoyne interests are not yet complete, but are progressing rapidly." OFM/DFM subsequently states that the outstanding issue related to the effect of the realignment and associated safety measures on the car-parking provision of the Everton Complex, and states that technical drawings would be complete within a few days to identify whether or not any problem would arise.

24 March 2002:

CRUA complains that promises to complete the relevant technical drawings are being repeatedly broken, and that the process again appears to be going nowhere.

27 March 2002:

OFM/DFM presents a sketch for comment before the technical drawings are prepared.

28 March 2002:

CRUA issues a full response to sketches, and repeats the request for urgent completion of technical drawings. OFM/DFM responds by saying that forthcoming holidays would impact, and also that MLA's would be briefed "over the next few days".

29 March 2002:

OFM/DFM circulates the final design brief, including the requirements as outlined by all relevant parties during the consultation process. The relevant parties included Glenbryn, lower Ardoyne, Everton Centre, Everton Day Centre, DRD Road Service and OFM/DFM.

11 April 2002:

OFM/DFM reports that the technical drawings are still not complete.

15 April 2002:

OFM/DFM reports that the technical drawings are to be completed later in the week.

17 April 2002:

OFM/DFM confirms that consultants are now drawing up final designs, including 3-D model of the various fences and walls.

23 April 2002:

Final design (in accordance with design brief) received.

24 April 2002:

CRUA responds with acceptance of final design.

26 April 2002:

OFM/DFM undertakes to provide details of ''progress on the timing issue''.

29 April 2002:

OFM/DFM reports that there are issues about sight-lines and the pace of community dialogue. CRUA responds with a request to specify the issue about sight-lines, and reminds OFM/DFM that there is no linkage between community dialogue and the safety package. To date, no response has been received.

7 May 2002:
OFM/DFM confirms that further meetings with Ardoyne interests are scheduled that day. Feedback is to be given to First Minister and Deputy First Minister, and a response to be issued on 8 May 2002.

9 May 2002:
OFM/DFM confirms that several meetings have taken place with Ardoyne interests, and information fed back to FM/DFM. However, as both FM and DFM have been in Derry, no response document has been prepared. OFM/DFM representative subsequently attends a CRUA meeting at the request of the committee, and in the absence of any new information is informed that the process is now all but exhausted.

10th May 2002:
A public meeting is held in Wheatfield Primary School with local MP Nigel Dodds, Billy Hutchinson MLA, Frazer Agnew MLA, Fred Cobain MLA and Councillor Nelson McCausland and the members of CRUA at which it was discussed what people felt in the area. A press statement was read to the press following this. Margaret McClenaghan SF also commented on UTV saying that the Glenbryn Residents had put forward a proposal through a third party - but is this not what they had signed up to on 23rd November and this really spoke volumes as Glenbryn residents had not put the proposal forward it was initiated by OFMDFM. But is this why they were saying no to the package; because Protestants had the audacity to come up with a possible solution to the Ardoyne Road dispute. Looks like it!

14th May 2002:

Lower Ardoyne community reps went to Stormont to meet Mr Trimble and Mr Durken to outline any problems they had with community safety or community dialogue. The community reps from Upper Ardoyne attended later that night. When asked what are the people of Ardoyne unhappy about, Mr Trimble replied "We do not know all the issues because not all the catholic reps were in attendance tonight. When asked why he replied, "members of the Ardoyne Focus Group could not attend as they had not met themselves beforehand", this only endorsed the feeling by those in Upper Ardoyne that the community reps in Lower Ardoyne were not interested in coming to an agreement.

17th May 2002:

A proposal was faxed to all stakeholders from OFM/DFM and both communities were given one week to respond with any justified changes.

18th - 20th May 2002:

Full copies of the proposals from OFM/DFM were delivered to every house in Upper Ardoyne so residents could see for themselves the proposals and voice their opinion to the content.

22nd May 2002:

A public meeting took place in Wheatfield School to give all residents a chance to air their views and to make a decision regarding the acceptance or decline of the proposals. Many residents raised issues they had regarding both the logistics of the proposals or the integrity of the First and Deputy First Minister. After discussions it was decided to take "a leap of faith" and accept the proposals.

23rd May 2002:

A public meeting was held in Lower Ardoyne and Gerard McGuigan spoke to the media saying: **BBC NI** - *Speaking after a meeting on Thursday, a spokesman for the Ardoyne residents said they could not accept the proposals for road re-alignment and a security wall. Gerard McGuigan said the proposals would isolate Holy Cross Girls' primary school from the community which it served. He said: "We don't want anything going across the road after what the children have been through which further isolates the school and increases tensions. "We would rather sit down with those people, agree a situation that both communities can live with and try and build some trust, but that's not happening".*

Should people not ask, then why then did community representatives from Ardoyne join in with consultations from January to May 2002 at all?

And remember the quote earlier from the letter to Nigel Dodds MP – "neither community will be permitted to veto developments which we consider essential to the successful implementation of the agreed package" It is blatantly obvious they felt they were essential or they wouldn't have taken the time to suggest them or to commend them in the first place – Certainly sounds like VETO to me.

BBC NI - Meanwhile, PUP assembly member Billy Hutchinson has said "Nationalists never intended to agree the deal, which also involved talks between the two sides. He said: "They have rejected it because it's a strategy from Republicans to make sure Protestants get it tight in north Belfast," he insisted. "It's about driving Protestants out of their homes".

7th June 2002: A further set of proposals were sent to all parties with amendments and No decision about the community safety and the security wall. There are further meetings to be scheduled with both communities to try to meet an agreement. Sadly people feel it is not fair that they have to ask their attackers to

13th June 2002:

Officials from OFM/DFM attended a committee meeting of CRUA to try to get them to compromise once again, they came from the stance that they had met with lower Ardoyne that afternoon and at this meeting those involved told the government officials that the concerns of the Upper Ardoyne community were being exaggerated to hype up the situation. This infuriated members of CRUA as the statistics spoke for themselves.

24th June 2002:

A public meeting was called due to NO response from OFM/DFM regarding the commended package; residents were becoming frustrated and angry that their safety was being compromised. It was perceived that due to the intense frustration that the protest could be re-ignited. Fortunately that night, after major discussion, the public were adamant that they should not let the powers that be in Lower Ardoyne, turn their concerns into a Holy Cross School issue it was unanimous that the protest should not return to the Ardoyne Road at this time and other avenues of protest should be investigated.

28th June 2002:

OFMDFM send a document which stated that independent arbitrators be assigned to work with both communities which does nothing only undermine any confidence anyone in the Protestant community had in

Mr Trimble and Mr Durken to lead this country. Feelings were that here we go again another process with no conclusion as there had been so many times before. A recommendation was to be submitted before end of July if all parties meet before then.

2nd August 2002: CRUA met with the arbitrators to raise their issues of concern

8th August 2002:

The arbitrators responded by email to say the following: "This is just to let you know that yesterday we submitted our report and recommendation to the First Minister and Deputy First Minister. As they are both on holidays, it may be some time before we can meet with them about this. Following such a meeting we expect to report back to your respective groups. Thank you again for your participation in this process."

Sadly at the time of this book going to print there has still been no outcome and no full implementation of the apparent promised package. Throughout the full process the protracted use of semantics by OFM/DFM has done nothing but confuse, frustrate and demoralise this struggling community in Upper Ardoyne.

Chapter 11
Eleven

Ongoing low-key intimidation - The ongoing saga

This community faces a chronic and serious threat to its safety, and in effect we must now face an extremely disturbing fact, that we may never have the security and protection we deserve as legitimate and valued citizens of this country

December 2001, three young schoolboys heading to school out of the top of Ardoyne Road and along the Ballysillan road - obscenities were shouted at them as a car flew past them and then they were followed and attacked by the same two men with large screwdrivers. It was only due to members of the public responding immediately to this, that the two men were apprehended in the Catholic Ardoyne district and charges have been brought, one of them in the post office (Royal Mail) uniform. (Did the Trade Union come out and condemn this sectarian attack)

7th January 2002, a young nationalist came up into Hesketh Road where a wreath was hung in commemoration to a young father and taxi driver, Trevor Kells who was murder in cold blood as he did a day's work in December 2000. The youth pulled the wreath from its position and ripped it up just as the bullets that killed Trevor had ripped that young family apart just over a year ago. After his act of desecration the young man ran to the side of Father Troy who stood at the interface with a number of others. Residents although very angry knew that this was an act of provocation and held back their anger and went to report the incident to the police.

Later that day there was a number of incidents between parents and residents but the final straw came when a crowd of nationalist men stood at the corner of Alliance Avenue and the Ardoyne Road, people thought they were there because of the incident in the morning with the wreath. A group of adults coming out of Holy Cross School marched down the Ardoyne Road, (keeping in mind this was after 3pm and the parents were coming out of the school they would obviously of had children with them BUT there were no children).

At the same time, there was a meeting in the community house with a delegation from OFM/DFM and CRUA. Three men left the community house and were walking up the Ardoyne Road. Both groups would now have to pass each other, but one of the parents spat at one of the residents and he responded by hitting out at them. At once, as if by remote control up came the crowd of approx. 50 men and started ripping off fences and attacking houses, the alarm siren was set off and Protestant residents came running to the sound of that all too familiar scream that meant another attack. The Republican propaganda machine went into action and the media covered the Holy Cross School being attacked by 50 loyalists men and how they had come into the school to attack the kids on their way home from school. The school headmistress later admitted that this was not a true account of what had happened. Sinn Fein representatives were on the media saying that this was started to re-launch the protest but residents at this point still had some confidence in the community safety package for their area and didn't want to go back down the road of the protest to submit to another's agenda. It later unfolded that Nationalists had booked tickets had been booked to go to Westminster/Downing Street to protest against the "Blockade against the children of Holy Cross" yet there had been no protest since 23rd November 2001 and this was now the 9th January 2002. Sadly their attempt to restart a protest which had delivered much in terms of victimhood and sympathy votes, did not work.

Saturday 3rd May 2002 brought a clash of the Scottish Football giants Rangers and Celtic a sure sign that whichever team won or lost there would be clashes between fans as there had been over many years. At approx. 2.30pm 3 committee members of CRUA were speaking to a journalist from Germany when three kids were riding their bikes on the road of

"Upper Ardoyne". Sure enough this was a sign to those "over the wall" that once again Upper Ardoyne was left open to attack. Within minutes the road was covered in about 30 - 40 young people firing golf balls and bricks up the road, but they were not to know that they had indeed proved our point to the reporter that Upper Ardoyne was under constant attack. The police came and agreed to requests to keep static police units there from 4.30 onwards when the football match would be due to end.

Later that day, the football match over residents went to drive down the Crumlin Road to town but could not pass due to the Nationalist crowds, which had just spurned out all over the Ardoyne shop fronts. Police and Army moved in to clear Twaddell Avenue of residents as the Nationalist crowd headed towards innocent Protestant homes. After about fi an hour the Nationalist crowd came up the Crumlin Road to the traffic lights just below Hesketh Road armed with bottles, brick golf balls, giant bolts with which they proceeded to attack the Protestant homes – at this entrance into Upper Ardoyne. Residents panicked and ran to defend their homes; the alarm was raised to alert whoever was about that there was an attack. Women and children screaming and senior citizens trying to help hold back the crowd of about 400 Nationalists, a small amount of police on the scene told residents "you may handle it, defend yourselves or die", at this point I myself was on the phone to Antrim Road police asking for resources to protect the Protestant homes from this attack, I was told that they were aware of the incident and they were already on route - I went on to inform him that the present police presence had said defend yourselves and warned him that if residents had to do this then the PSNI vehicles should not come in heavy handed and beat back the people trying to protect their homes. In the meantime two elderly men were hurt and had to be rushed to hospital with head injuries and I called for an ambulance, the police at that point came blasting down the road swaying into the residents and going out of their way to knock people down, the blood of the two men was everywhere and there were women and children screaming at what was going on. No one knew what to do for the best or how to calm the situation down; indeed should it ever have got to this stage I asked myself! The ambulances tried to come up the Crumlin Road to see to the injured which had grown now to 6 but the Nationalist crowd would not let them through so they had to turn around and come up the Ardoyne Road, but still the PSNI were driving their land rovers like bumper cars in a fairground, maybe Protestant lives to them are only part of a game. One resident claimed, "It took a full 30 minutes for the PSNI to respond to the first calls for help. And people asked why we protested! If only they lived here, wouldn't they know the real story?"

13th June 2002	Young widow living in Upper Ardoyne, whose husband was murdered by INLA 9 years ago, house was attacked in the middle of the night, smashing windows and paint-bombing both the inside and outside of the house
13th June 2002	Car entering Hesketh Road, Upper Ardoyne was attacked by male adolescents on their way to attend a nearby catholic secondary school – they had the bricks in their schoolbags – the owner/driver of the car has just started a football club in Upper Ardoyne to help divert young people from the interface

15th June 2002 The same young widow from 13th June incident receives a threat through the mail telling her "the next time it will be petrol bombs"

18th June 2002 Wheatfield Primary School (on the other side of the road from Holy Cross PS) receives a phone call from the Catholic Reaction Force

18th June 2002 A senior citizen from the Upper Ardoyne area is manhandled from Ardoyne shops while going to collect her old age pension, she was left distressed and disorientated in the street to find her way home

19th June 2002 Springfield Primary School – a Protestant primary school situated in a Nationalist area receives through the mail a threat from the Catholic Reaction Force

19th June 2002 Contractors threatened and walked off the site when installing CCTV on Ardoyne Roundabout/Twaddell Interface

20th June 2002 Suspect bomb left on Roundabout at Ardoyne/Twaddell Interface where CCTV contractors were working

20th June 2002 A female student standing at a bus stop on the Crumlin Road adjacent to Upper Ardoyne was

	surrounded harassed and had sectarian abuse hurled at her by approx 20 adolescent schoolboys from a nearby catholic boys school
21st June 2002	A married Couple both approx. 80 years receives threat through the mail from Catholic Reaction Force, saying their homes will be bombed
21st June 2002	A senior citizen living on her own in Twaddell Avenue receives threat through the mail from Catholic Reaction Force, saying her home will be bombed
21st June 2002	A woman aged 76 living on her own in Glenbryn Estate receives her second threat from Catholic Reaction Force, saying her home will be bombed
21st June 2002	Nationalist attack an orange parade in the Duncairn area of North Belfast – a parade route which was passed by the parades commission
22nd June 2002	Continuity IRA issues a death threat to contractors installing CCTV to identify rioters etc. Via North Belfast News – "Anyone installing or maintaining CCTV in Ardoyne area will be executed"

22nd June 2002 Continuity IRA issues threat to contractors who are making any attempt to build a wall at Ardoyne Road near Holy Cross School, "We are making it clear that we will attack any contractor who attempts to build any such wall".

The Residents spokesman stated, "The guns, bullets and death-threats are back. Having watched as community representatives spent 7 months formulating a safety package for the Ardoyne interface, Republicans are obviously shattered that they have not got everything their own way as they expected. So they have decided to re-deploy their special negotiating tactic - terrorism."

A leading community worker stated on 24th June 2002,

"The ongoing disregard of violent facts sends a chilling message to loyalists and is leading this province back to conflict where it will leave loyalist residents no other option but to protect their area from any serious sectarian acts of aggression or further sectarian attacks. The recent upsurge of sectarian intimidation and threats cannot be tolerated in a peaceful society and it is not right to concede the Human Rights of Protestant residents to appease their aggressors.

PM Tony Blair says that this is the most successful peace process in the world but it needs a little help at the moment. But lets be honest it is dead in the water and an incredibly modest amount of the Protestant community have any trust in it, when all their vital needs and safety concerns are being ignored."

He also suggested, "*Something needs to be done immediately to alleviate the frustration of the people who are feeling under siege and under threat of intimidation and it should not be left until things get to boiling point where frustration leads people to act out of character.*

Many people believe that the Good Friday Agreement is finished, ceasefires have been broken, deadlines extended and rules changed to suit the whim of the day – this is no way to rule a country."

24th June 2002 - A public meeting at a local venue lasted just over an hour, and was attended by several hundred residents who expressed growing impatience at the lack of progress on the package which was commended by the First and Deputy First Ministers on 17 May. There was discussion about the suspension of their protest due to the previous week's events – it was decided not to return to the protest at this time.

Residents' spokesman Mark Coulter said: 'The residents were clear that their protest was never about a school, but about community safety, and they were adamant that they should not do anything which could be misconstrued as directed at a school.'

Ongoing orchestration and intimidation of residents in North Belfast is continuing at an alarming rate throughout the summer months and on the lead up to the main 12th of July parade in Belfast. The following excerpt outlines a statement from Assistant Chief Inspector Alan McQuillan released on 11th July, many believe that this was a tactic used by the PSNI to highlight and divert conflict from the Ardoyne shop fronts on 12th July 2002 and that by releasing this statement it was hoped that the sting would be taken out of any potential riot situations that would replicate the year before when over 100 police officers were beaten and injured one of which was struck by a hatchet.

2001

Assistant Chief Constable Alan McQuillan said: *"People cannot come out and say they want human rights and then decide they are going to have pick 'n' mix rights where they are going to choose what rights they have and what rights they deny to others.*

"Our job in this is to enforce the Parades Commission determination and to do everything we could to ensure that things pass off peacefully."

2002

"Police have uncovered hundreds of petrol bombs being made ready in north Belfast ahead of the Twelfth of July parades.

Mr McQuillan said: "We have very clear information that large numbers of Republican youths are being bussed into the area by Republican paramilitaries and that large quantities of petrol bombs and acid bombs are being manufactured.

"We are saying that a Republican paramilitary organisation is clearly organising and is directly behind this," **Mr McQuillan said."** Ananova – 11th July 2002

A local resident from Upper Ardoyne who followed the small feeder parade home on the night of the 12th July 2002 gave the following account:

"I was with my young 9 year old son enjoying the 12th of July parade; we followed the bands and Orangemen from central Belfast up towards home enjoying the festive music and entertainment. As we came towards Ardoyne there were rumours of gunmen in Ardoyne, people were very frightened but as there was no other route we had no other choice but to go through to get home. The PSNI grouped the small parade together with the followers and surrounded them to try to give them free, secure passage past the Ardoyne shop fronts. Crowds of Nationalists had came from the back streets of Ardoyne to shout abuse at us as we walked past they wailed bottles, bricks and fireworks at the group of which most were children and teenagers who had followed the parade for the near 14 mile return journey. I was behind a guy from the community who had a video camera and behind the police cordon of landrover's, grown men were caught on video pretending to shoot at us when they realised they were being filmed they tried to cover up their faces; what drives them to get on like this. The noise from the 500+ protesting crowd was deafening and the kids were screaming with fear. Some people were hit and injured with the objects that were thrown, I do not understand why these people came out to do this, they cannot be offended because it is a row of shops and only a few houses; where did all the crowds come from and why? Catholic areas have their festivities when they hold their 'fleadh' and there is none of this nonsense. Live and let live that is what I say, but if they wanted to stop me as a Protestant walking through that area they have succeeded as I will never take my child through that area again, they have done nothing only created another no-go area with no tolerance for another's culture, I believe they have a right to celebrate their culture but all I deserve is parity of esteem – My family should be allowed to celebrate ours."

21st July –2002 – Many homes came under attack in the early hours of the morning (approx. 4.30am) on Ardoyne Road and Glenbryn Park. A white car was seen at the scene where men took baseball bats and stool legs from the boot of the car and proceeded to attack local homes. One woman had just moved out the night before after 13 years with her young son as she could take no more. *"I did not want to move,"* cried the woman, *"but I could not stick any more attacks. Last night they even painted my poor dog who was in the vacant house as I had not moved all my furniture out. My son and I were sleeping on the floor of the new house when we heard the racket, they would have killed us if we had of been in that house."*

21st July 2002 - The UDA admitted murdering a young catholic father on July 21 in the Whitewell area of Belfast after a series of attacks in the north of the city; it is believed this was sparked by an indiscriminate Republican gun attack at the peaceline at Ardoyne which seriously injured a young Protestant father.

Throughout July 2002 and becoming greater in August 2002 there has been a more sustained rate of shootings, attacks, sectarian hit and run crimes in North Belfast against the Protestant community; day and night on an almost daily basis; although I have spoken of how this is proven through the statistics of those fleeing their homes it is now happening simultaneously and in disturbingly excessive numbers. These attacks cannot be sustained by these communities and no-one can even attempt to know what it feels like to live under such conditions. I have to ask; why is this being allowed to happen? Why can we not have a police force with the power to deal with situations and implement the law? Why is it acceptable to have terrorism on our streets? I hear many of you saying we have the law with the PSNI on our streets but this is diluted and their hands are tied, they need to be a force that can go into both communities and implement the law not just one!

Conflict is back on the streets of North Belfast with a vengeance and to the horror of many who are seriously feeling let down by the local government, the NIO and that of Westminster.

A local community worker in Upper Ardoyne said, The community of Upper Ardoyne feel very negative about the input of the NI Executive and would state that community leaders and Public Representatives were engaged to help solve issues in North Belfast and they did so with sincere commitment, but the complacency of David Trimble and Mark Durkan to make decisions regarding safety measures, created a vacuum that could only be filled by **ALL** paramilitaries revisiting conflict on the streets, which in turn manifested itself in the current volatile situation.

*"It is obvious that **Sinn Fein** will say anything to anyone at anytime, simply to suit their own purposes. How can we have any confidence in them?"*
David Trimble 23rd July 2002 – Belfast Telegraph

The above statement could be quite confidently be reiterated by the Upper Ardoyne Community - only it would go as follows:

"It is obvious that, **FM David Trimble and DFM Mark Durkan** will say anything to anyone at anytime, simply to suit their own purposes. How can we have any confidence in them?"

Protestant residents also feel that double standards are being shown throughout the world including the south of Ireland, Cathy a resident said "There is no way the USA would accept Osama Bin Laden as their Minister for Education; And in the south of Ireland elections it was stated they didn't want Sinn Fein in the high ranks of their government; but we have to accept it! How do these people expect us to accept terrorists in government and they won't and don't accept the same.

By BBC NI political editor Mark Devenport - *Sinn Fein hopes to make major gains during the Irish election. The party might be in an influential position after the votes are counted, and the shape of a future Irish coalition is being decided. That possibility prompted senior figures from Mr Ahern's Fianna Fail to discount a governmental role for Sinn Fein because of its association with "a private army", otherwise known as the Provisional IRA.*

These exchanges south of the border prompted some to scratch their heads, look at Sinn Fein's ministers in charge of Northern Ireland's schools and hospitals, and wonder if they were witnessing a case of double standards.

Positively, community representatives of Upper Ardoyne and many other interfaces have tried to take on responsibility for their community needs and lack of support for community infrastructure in these forgotten areas. But this can only be done with the support of those in higher places of responsibility who can lead by example and encourage the good, honest and genuine attempts to resolve issues. Where is our strong leadership!

If a seed of lettuce will not grow, we do not blame the lettuce. Instead, the fault lies with us for not having nourished the seed properly.
Buddhist proverb.

Chapter 12
Twelve

The Uniting of Protestant interfaces

> Snowflakes are one of nature's most fragile things, but just look what they can do when they stick together
>
> ~ Vista M. Kelly ~

The following statements is in no way the full account of what these communities have had to suffer but they are a small taste of what other Protestant communities are going through and the horrendous events that are creating the sense of extreme frustration within them and so encouraging all Protestant interfaces to identify with each others evident concerns.

Torrens

Torrens is another small Protestant enclave surrounded by a catholic area, with what must definitely be the worse housing conditions in North Belfast – although a new redevelopment programme has been implemented. A fence designed to prevent Nationalist youths from attacking Protestant homes in the Torrens estate in the Oldpark area, remains incomplete months after workmen walked off site. The fence was started but partially demolished in the dark of night by a crowd of Nationalists who arrived with hammers, pickaxes, chisels and various other implements. Then when workmen returned to complete the job, they were approached by a number of people including a Sinn Fein member, and they walked off site a short time later. They have never returned. This lack of security claimed two latest victims, who sadly were; a young disabled child hit with a brick and a young 3 year old beaten up by a group of youths wearing Celtic shirts. Again forgotten children in this conflict!

The steadfast faithful voluntary committee here have endeavoured to work for good relations in the area and this has just lately been paid off by them securing a new community centre for the residents. But even this is coming under attack.

Whitecity

A small Protestant estate in North Belfast, who again has had its fair share of conflict, intimidation and sectarian hatred thrown at it for many years. Indeed it has reached the point where persistent nightly riots have occurred and residents have been forced to move out. They have no access to shopping facilities or even the nearest bus stop without coming under attack from their neighbours. Again this is a community with very little community infrastructure, although within the last months a new centre has been built ran by volunteers but with no paid workers in place. 4th September 2001 brought a real sadness to this community and indeed throughout North Belfast, as they feel they have seen blatant sectarianism in all its shame; a young lad, Thomas MacDonald, lost his life when a Catholic woman, a mother, in a car and her passengers allegedly drove directly towards the youth and killed him outright. Thomas was 16 years old; the woman is now charged with murder and is on bail awaiting trial. She denies the charges. RUC believed there could be a sectarian motive, the case is pending.

This small area feeling under siege by the large Catholic population around it and saw some of the worst riots over the past year, again it is Protestant residents who flee their homes.

Limestone Road/North Queen Street

This area has been highlighted as one of the largest trouble-spots in North Belfast with constant riot situations which are known by the residents to be orchestrated by well known Republicans. One onlooker witnessed an attack by youths from the Catholic Newington area that ferociously attacked Protestant Hallidays Road where there were no residents on the street. Security forces were called and when the sirens from the police vehicles were heard, a loud whistle was blown and all the attackers ran back into the houses in their own area. By the time the police had arrived residents from the Protestant enclave had came out to see what was going on and the police believed them to be the perpetrators and engaged in attempting to arrest innocent residents. Little did they know that the whole show had been caught on video footage from start to end!

This is another area that has seen its fair share of recent tragedies where young men have lost their lives due to the attacks and ongoing trauma associated with living in this volatile interface area – the latest being a young father who was mown down by a Nationalist car.

The ongoing shooting attacks from the Nationalist community are proven in the fact that there have been many casualties on the Protestant side but none on the Nationalist side. Dedicated community workers in this area again give their time voluntarily; and for many years, to try to deliver to the people a better way of life – without sectarian hatred. But this proves very difficult when again it is confirmed in statistics that the exodus from homes is on the Protestant side of the divide.

Cambria Street

This street has witnessed frequent ongoing attacks on senior citizens homes that are close to the Crumlin Road interface which also links with Ardoyne, with windows being constantly smashed and paint-bombed putting invariable fear into these elderly people. Throughout the summer of 2001 this area saw extensive riot situations and so seen reason to hold nightly protests to highlight their concerns at a man who was dragged into Brookfield Mill which had been taken over by an unruly Nationalist crowd. At first police would not respond to go in and rescue the abducted man which led to a more sustained attack on the man and him being left severely beaten and near death.

A new community group formed to distract young people from the interface with diversionary activities but again this dedicated band of volunteers have had very little help or support to expand and develop as they have worked to keep the area quiet; and with very little credit for their successes and voluntary contributions.

Lower Oldpark/Manor Street

A community left with many housing difficulties as it has watched its neighbours intimidate and threaten the residents out of the estate. This was a relatively new estate built to replace older homes in the area but it is believed that when the area was being rebuilt many parts of the residential area was replaced with commercial properties causing another flashpoint area. Even though there is a massive peace wall erected to protect homes. But the area still is under threat from sporadic attacks and most homes close to the peaceline are vacant. More recently a pensioner escaped death when only one of three petrol bombs destined for his Clifton Park Avenue home, ignited. It is proposed to redevelop the area. There are dedicated workers in this area who have worked for years devoting their time to calming interface tensions.

Interfaces unite

It is a well-known fact that interface conflict over the past year in North and East Belfast has been the worst for many years. Indeed statistics show that `11 people in North Belfast have been shot and a further 5 in East Belfast including children – All Protestant except 3! Only through the gift of God; has no-one been killed whilst the many live rounds of gunfire shot up the Ardoyne Road, on many occasions. These incidents are either denied or there are weak attempts to justify the use of live ammunition against innocent people. Or the new tactic of course; "Blame it on the UDA," no-one will ask questions. But the evident strike marks are there to prove differently.

Loyalist paramilitaries do not deny their involvement in these clashes and indeed some come openly out and put their hands up to it; but Republicans have relinquished any responsibility for the outbreaks of violence in these areas – yet don't the statistics speak for themselves? Protestants are fleeing their homes in Glenbryn, Cluan Place, Torrens, Lower Oldpark, Whitecity, Limestone, Ardoyne Road and now Hesketh; to name but a few. It is clear to see that if Nationalists/Republicans can not take responsibility for their actions then they will never be seen to have morals, principals or integrity which will constantly lead to further mistrust and indigenous contempt for each other.

> ***Whilst there is a perception of a concerted attempt to eradicate the culture** of the Protestant community, there will always be the feeling of being 'pushed out into the cold.'*
>
> *We must create **an underlying aim within Northern Ireland of promoting cultural understanding, tolerance and a sense of identity through respect for each others culture and not become so engrossed in one culture that other cultures and the people in them become unimportant or morally questioned. Attitudes must be challenged and a foundation set to address issues of cultural arrogance i.e., belief in the superiority of one culture over another.***

BEYOND THE RED GAUNTLET

One positive aspect that has happened throughout North Belfast and even East Belfast to a certain extent is that Protestant interfaces were feeling alike and as they realised they were not alone in their conflict at interfaces and flashpoint areas, they began to unite, contacting each other in times of trouble or just for moral support. But in any terms there was a dramatic shift in how Protestants were altering their ways of coping. Many of these communities had come through internal turmoil themselves but now found that their gift of diversity had to be harnessed and used in the most positive manner it could, for their latest united struggle for safety and security in their communities.

The North Belfast Action Project created by OFMDFM to engage with the communities of North Belfast highlighted the fact that communities needed to work together and form partnerships for support and strategic planning for the future of their communities. Previously this would have been a challenge to many but after the past year of mayhem this seemed to evolve naturally if even on an ad hoc basis. But it must be recognised by those in power that there is a real difference in community infrastructure between the Protestant and Catholic communities and as such issues in relation to parity of esteem must be dealt with or there will always be inequality.

Although still in its infancy, Protestant communities are learning to communicate, to facilitate and endorse each others work to recreate positive, vibrant communities once again. As many times in their history they have had to unite, I am sure they will do so again when it comes to the final crunch and they can take no more – and they will be like the snowflake - a powerful force when they stick together.

Chapter 13
Thirteen

The words of the people

A chapter dedicated to the people of Upper Ardoyne to have their voice and feelings heard - the voice of the disenfranchised.

BEYOND THE RED GAUNTLET

B A Foster – Long Term Resident/Voluntary Community Worker

Growing up as a child in Glenbryn, I remember when at night, lights had to be out and we had to lie on the freezing cold floors. There were ongoing shooting attacks and it was believed if the house was in darkness then Republicans wouldn't have a target to shoot at.

I remember playing in a garden with friends facing the Jolly Rodger Social Club (which has been closed now for many years) when Republicans came up and shot a number of people including my grandmother; I remember the times that hundreds of Nationalists would burst through the peaceline and attack the homes and residents who lived there; I also recall the many times being taunted and physically abused when I went to the Everton secondary school on the Ardoyne Road. At lunch times we had to make sure we were in groups before we could venture to the Ardoyne shops so we could buy our lunch as in a group it was much harder for us to be attacked. On many occasions I witnessed Protestant children being badly beaten up with adult shoppers looking on and not trying to stop the attack. There were no police, press or government interested in protecting or supporting us - the government's response was to close the school and now it is used for people with disabilities. The people in this building still come under constant attack by ongoing trouble at the Alliance Avenue/Ardoyne Road interface. There are constant attacks on the roof tiles of this centre, hoping that the continued expense will make the government tenants move elsewhere. Where is the help and aid for those people in this Centre who probably don't care what a catholic or Protestant is? I feel if the government fail to secure the Ardoyne Road, these vital services for disabled adults will also have to close. As if that is not bad enough there are constant bomb scares at the front of the

Building on the Crumlin Road, restricting their access to the building at all. Republicans have also used the car-park of the building to launch attacks on the Protestant houses in Hesketh Road. Where is the security for these residents? Is this a Strategy by elements in Ardoyne to have this land for houses or to stop the bands/parades from walking down the Crumlin Road?

Fortunately with the scenes I have seen and the trauma I have endured, I've grown up into adulthood not too mentally scarred but certainly full of vivid tragic memories. I often have thought to myself why the government, police, press are not helping the people of Upper Ardoyne, people were moving out in large numbers and all the government agencies seemed to be encouraging them.

I helped form the (GGCI) Greater Glenbryn Community Initiative in 1997 which empowered local residents to fight all the opposing bodies, for the 'right to life' and 'freedom to live free from intimidation' for all our residents. We got off to a great start by forming an agreement with the Housing Executive to rebuild Glenbryn Park and Glenbryn Drive. We worked to get all the Houses on the Ardoyne Road allocated and we succeeded (except for one flat) but now that's all gone again! We even had agreement from the NIO (Northern Ireland Office) to build a peaceline along the back of the Houses in Glenbryn Park. We also agreed with them (1997) Security Gates along the Ardoyne Road at the junction of Alliance Avenue as the number of attacks were unbelievably high. In one week there were four bomb scares at the first block of Protestant houses at the interface on the Ardoyne Road. Terrorists would casually walk up and knock on the residents windows and tell them they had five minutes to get out; I ask you to think about this! What would you do? Would you feel safe living there? Would you want your family living there? When Sinn Fein heard about the agreement on the security gates it was rumoured that it was Glenbryn resident's intention was to have the gates closed all the time. This was pure falsehood and propaganda. We had said from the start it would be the responsibility of police to open & close the gates in times of conflict. The Ardoyne Road residents only wanted the reassurance that if trouble started then the gates could be closed to let thing calm down. Residents would then feel safe to live in their homes. But Sinn Fein had another agenda; they went to the NIO and RUC and got them to review the situation for a few months, when surprise surprise! The attacks from Nationalist Ardoyne stopped almost immediately; so the gates and the peaceline at the backs of the houses were scrapped. Residents were disgusted; they felt alone, frustrated and now legitimately believed that no-one cared.

The GGCI tried hard and started working with the youth in the area. We got a two bedroom flat which we turned into a community house, the kids just started coming in wanting somewhere they could sit and talk and have a cup of tea. This was a great success we changed their minds and helped them to feel safe standing on that part of the Ardoyne Road again. They even got to the stage were if there were catholic kids standing at the top of Alliance Avenue, instead of hitting out at each other they started accepting each others right to be there. The attacks on upper Ardoyne started to escalate again following the Murder of Trevor Kell. I wonder who has it on their conscious; that if there had been gates on the Ardoyne Road this young family man might still be alive. There were other shootings where people were injured but coincidentally did not loss their lives. In January 2001 the attacks got so vicious that we couldn't risk the lives of the kids and had to stop them coming into the community house. This left the kids with nothing; no one to guide them; leaving them to defend themselves and the area. We had worked so hard but I believe Republicans had ruined all our hard work.

The final straw was the incident that started the protest on the Ardoyne Road. Apparently no one cared about the kids who lived on the Ardoyne Road who couldn't come out to play or be safe walking a short distance up to their school. All the people seen were the kids who had to use the road for 10 minutes in the morning and 10 minutes in the afternoon. What about the children who have lived there for years; 24 hours a day; who have lost everything; and have received nothing; not even their safety!

Now in August 2002 I feel worse; stressed and frustrated as the government, police and especially Trimble/Durkan have let us down with broken promises. I can't count the number of families who have had to leave their homes & community permanently to live somewhere where their children are safe to play or walk the streets. I feel for years we done the work of the government and police and this is how they repay us; they didn't care! It is their moral duty to protect all residents and STOP the attacks not just for Nationalist Ardoyne. How many times are they going to make us go through this? **And WHY?**

Davy Wright – One of latest victims of attacks on homes in North Belfast

On the 22nd of July 2002 at 02.05 am. I heard an almighty crash coming from downstairs and a voice yelling "orange bastards". Then there was a screeching of tyres and a car speeding off up the hill. When I got downstairs

BEYOND THE RED GAUNTLET

I was met with a devastating sight. Our front window had been smashed and glass was everywhere. I heard the commotion outside and was met by a few of my neighbours soon realising that the two pensioners next door to me had also been attacked. I immediately rang 999 and informed the police, who said they would respond.

I waited over twenty minutes and the police still did not arrive. By this time my wife and the two pensioners were hysterical and some friends did their best to consol them. I rang 999 again and by this time, with my temper near to breaking point. I had an exchange with the officer on line. I asked him if 999, was an emergency number and he refused to answer the question. In my opinion this was an emergency and the police should have arrived by now as the police station was only 5 minutes from my home. Then the phone rang and my wife answered it. It was the policeman I was previously talking to and he informed my wife that due to my attitude they may not attend this incident.

He stated that a similar incident had happened in Catholic Ligoniel and that when they were finished with that, they would see to us. My wife told him that if we were Catholics, the police would have been here immediately and she put down the phone. Five minutes later, the same car with the perpetrators still in it, passed by our houses and went on to attack other houses in the area. The police arrived 45 minutes after the incident, took details of what had happened and left without even the assurance that they would remain in the area or indeed that security would be steeped up in this area. If they had arrived sooner they would have been able to catch or a least give chase to these thugs thereby saving some other householder the anguish and fear suffered by my wife, our neighbours and myself.

The next day I contacted the local television stations and all the local press and gave details of what had occurred the previous night and not one of them took up the story. Later in the day I learnt that 22 Protestant houses had been attacked in a similar way that night and again none of them received media coverage. But, all the Catholic houses that had been attacked had their MP's, Councillors and all the local media falling over each other to report their incidents.

During the Upper Ardoyne resident's dispute, on one occasion I counted 120 police land rovers in that area. They were there to allow Catholic "parents" to walk their children to Holy Cross School. Again the media fell over themselves to cover events. The truth, if it is allowed to be aired is that the "parents" consisted of mothers, fathers, uncles, brothers, sisters, cousins and the odd IRA/INLA man thrown in for good measure. With all these land rovers and police personnel available it is not unreasonable for me to expect one land rover to respond when I need help; but then again I am a Protestant and therefore do not afford the same response from the security forces of this country. If Catholics claim to be second-class citizens, then what am I?

Protestant people in Northern Ireland (other than interface areas) need a wake-up call! Do they not see what is happening right in front of them? We are systematically being persecuted, divided, our culture eroded, and if we do nothing to help this we will be eradicated.

When a Catholic person is killed or injured, when Catholic property, again specifically churches are attacked it is always "sectarian". When rioting occurs and Catholics are involved we never hear the word "scum" but we have heard them called "excited youths". Protestants on the other hand are getting blamed regardless and have on many occasion been tarred with the word scum.

A major question, which must be answered, is why there can only be "dissident Republicans" but never "dissident loyalists"? Throughout the history of the world conflict and war the victors have one thing in common; to win they must divide their enemy.

Two sayings spring to mind, the first being 'United we stand, divided we fall' and the second being 'the truth hurts.' Open your eyes!

Survivor of Terrorism, Who has lived at both sides of this Interface in Ardoyne

The Ardoyne road - **why?**

A community that was left with no alternative! Other than to take to the streets and protest!

From Hesketh to Glenbryn on to Alliance and Wheatfield, one thing is for sure the so-called peace agreement has brought nothing to these streets. There are many vacant, run-down houses and high rates of unemployment. Amongst its inhabitant's is the fear of what the night will bring and a genuine disbelief that 'the powers that be' cannot see behind the S F propaganda.

Day and daily this small isolated vulnerable community is attacked by

Republicans hell bent on driving them out of their homes and destroying their small community so that Republican Ardoyne can expand. [See Belfast Telegraph 14.08.02]. These attacks are relentless, happening both by day and night, even now in full view of CCTV cameras it still occurs because Republican Ardoyne know that nothing will be done to those who control and orchestrate the attacks.

Look around you on the Ardoyne road look at the grills on the windows, grills that have been there for 19 years not for the last 18 months; see the empty houses - are these homes of attackers or are these homes of those who are being attacked. Government, journalists/Media and the security forces need to look within their own houses and put them in order first, before telling this small isolated and vulnerable community how it should behave.

Not one TV crew, not one journalist or human rights representative has looked behind what has happened on the Ardoyne road, to find out why a small community stood against the rest of the world or that's how it seemed for them at the time. Take a close look at the people, who stood on that road, they were made up of pensioners, woman with young families and young men who may have had hope for the future of their community but this was kicked and beaten out of them. The police, media and the government left us with no alternative so residents went on to the streets in an attempt through 'peaceful protest', to save their community from its ultimate destruction by Republican Ardoyne and I was proud to stand with them, proud to be asked to represent them on the CRUA committee.

We tried to stay within the law at all times, keeping the protest as peaceful as possible under very trying circumstances. But this was made virtually impossible because of a decision made by the Chief Constable R Flannigan (at that time) to push the Republican movement under the guise of parents, of Holy cross children, up the Ardoyne road. This decision was made and announced in the middle of the summer, long before the return to school, making it impossible for talks to take place; After all at why talk when the police, Secretary of State and Security minister had given a commitment to force people up the road no matter what.

To have to stand and watch as the police escort known murderers and bombers up the Ardoyne road past your homes, while you and the rest of your community are pushed into side streets and gardens, or told to go another route! Woman and pensioners beaten by the 'so called' forces of law and order; yes beaten! Even in their own gardens; pushed into their homes and not allowed to walk on there own streets. A wreath that had been put up by the widow of Mr T. Kell ripped down by a Republican, when neighbours complained to the police the Inspector told them it was provocative to have put the wreath up anyway! Was it not more provocative to have killed this father and husband in the first place, but then again we can not upset Republicans. It is not important that prods are being killed in these streets; after all, there is a peace process. BUT IS THERE? This community wants to know where it is and when will it take account of them and their needs.

As we stood shoulder to shoulder, we noticed the public representatives who came listened and stood with us, and I personally would like to thank Cllr Billy Hutchinson MLA, Cllr Nelson McCausland and Assembly Minister

Nigel Dodds MP and I would also ask the other public reps who were not there – Where were you when this community needed you most? We will remember at the ballot box.

And finally Trimble and Durkan, you have shirked your responsibilities to both communities and do not deserve the title of First Minister and Deputy First Minister of NI.

Andy Cooper – Voluntary Community Worker

The Ardoyne Road protest was an inevitable response to a repugnant attack on an unsuspecting and vulnerable community.

The greatest difficulty that faced the community was maintaining a peaceful and dignified protest especially when provoked by a Sinn Fein propaganda machine in overdrive or overkill. Add this to governmental intransigence or deliberate bias, either way it meant they would not deal with the initial problem.

The 3rd of September will only be remembered for the handful of crying school children and angry faces of protestors, that was what was designed for the world to see. You weren't meant to see the arrest of a blind man by riot police who had desperately tried to provoke a riot until then; the continual assaults by police officers who beat every man, woman and child off the Ardoyne Road; Nor did you see the hundreds of known armed IRA men given freedom to cause havoc on the Ardoyne Road; starting a riot, which police refused to respond to.

The world media also mysteriously missed Shankill bomber, Sean Kelly's message to the people of Hesketh of a repeat bombing campaign; maybe they were too busy being courted by Sinn Fein.

None of this excuses the actions of protestors, but it may shed some light on why Sinn Fein obtained their early propaganda coup. The British government civil servants believed that this was the best way to handle this situation, unlike Lower Ormeau and Garvaghy Road.

What we have seen in Loyalist Ardoyne is a failure of local government, national government and civil servants to act on their responsibilities. The only people to gain out of the brutalisation of our small community are politicians and paramilitaries. Neither the community, nor Holy Cross School have benefited from this governmental failure. The community to date have undelivered promises and Holy Cross dwindling numbers - Both scenarios do little to boost confidence in safety or security ever being dealt with, in a sensible or rational manner.

Hopefully when sectarianism is being eradicated by the British Government and the Northern Ireland Assembly, then high on their agenda will be the end of state sponsored sectarianism within our education system. Children are the seeds that we sow today for our future tomorrow. What sort of future are we giving our children when we carry out an age-old task of separating them from one another? This is the most blatant form of sectarianism we have, but it is never allowed to be questioned.

Bill Morris, Transport and General Workers Union (General Secretary), has already warned the British Government of its plan to increases the number of faith based schools in England as a "time bomb". He said "the plan to increase would lead to increased racial tension", maybe Mr. Morris looked at Northern Ireland's segregated education as an example.

William John Foster – Shankill Bomb Victim and Long Term Resident of Upper Ardoyne

I have been a resident of Upper Ardoyne since 1940's and always went out of my way to embrace the catholic community. Since being caught up in the Shankill Bomb seeing the horrific scenes before me that day; of men, women and children, being pulled from the mountains of filthy rubble; suffering the ongoing incursions into our community and now living under the constant fear of a murderous attack on the people here – I feel we deserve to demand security and community safety for our area. We live everyday now tolerating the attacks and shootings, verbal abuse and put down's because it has not been dealt with by the authorities. It has even become virtually acceptable because it happens every single day. Speaking from my own experience I feel as though I have been a victim in the past and now, in spite of everything, I still have to suffer this ongoing hatred by watching the perpetrator of the Shankill bomb casually walk up the Ardoyne Road and warn us of the next one which he says will be for us!. How long am I going to have to be the victim before it is acknowledged? How long do I have to suffer? And how long is it going to take before someone stops this vicious circle?

Gerry – A Long Term Resident of Upper Ardoyne

When I was first approached about the idea of staging a protest against Republican attacks in the area, I had to think long and hard as I didn't want to be involved in any protest where a child could be mentally or physically hurt.

BEYOND THE RED GAUNTLET

As a loyalist I still believe in the right of children, Catholic or Protestant and to the right to education in a peaceful environment. Having satisfied my own mind that this protest was against many Republican and bigoted parents who, by day abused our young on their daily trek up our end of the road and by night carried out sectarian attacks against our young and old, I decided to join and give my all to the protest.

I not only held these Republican thugs to blame, but also the media, Northern Ireland Office and the First and Deputy First Minister's; a lot of the blame lies with these people. The Protestant people have been left with no choice, no-one was interested in what was happening to our community it was nothing less than genocide; our people have been shot, bombed and physically beaten, our homes constantly attacked and our young mentally disturbed.

Our protest was not about any children, it was about the bigoted thugs who escorted them up the road, and on many occasion, they were not even the parents or relatives of any of these children. Instead they were hand picked Republicans with no other purpose than to provoke a reaction from the normally peaceful Protestant people.

I was there from the start to finish, at times things did turn nasty, one has to wonder why; where-in I feel the answer lies between the R.U.C./P.S.N.I. and their Sinn Fein counterparts. Chief Constable, Ronnie Flanagan, made a statement saying, he would not force his child through the protest as there was an alternative route, yet, he was quite content to let known IRA parents and non-parents to physically drag and sometimes beat those innocent children up that road, while they constantly shouted abuse and threats to the protesters, i.e. "it won't be long until we burn you orange bastards out".

What the media chose not to show the world was the infringement of our human rights, to live our lives in a peaceful society, and the right of our young to walk their own streets without fear being hemmed in to those same streets; and often to be late to school and coming home.

Why? - In order to facilitate those 'bullyboys' and women to parade their Republican hatred under our noses, talk about rubbing salt into wounds, anything to appease Sinn Fein. Had we wanted, we could have stopped this walk of shame, but this would have resulted in some of their children maybe being hurt, one child hurt would have been one too many. That is the real reason why we did not at any time resort to violence against those known Republicans on parade, even though we were under extreme provocation; for that I applaud the decency and concern of the Protestant people of the area. No one wanted to be protesting a minute longer than necessary, and when the so-called opportunity arose for what was believed to be a fair and equal settlement, the Protestant people embraced it.

The thought of living out their lives in peace had been their only wish, and now it seemed it was within their grasp. At the time of writing, I'm now feeling the First and Deputy First Ministers have betrayed this community, if this is the case, then they may rue the day they bowed to Republican pressure, for this community has come through too much to let any thug or friend of theirs in suit, shirt and tie to continue to try and walk all over them.

To finish, I ask everyone this question, what is the Republican agenda? When they agree to and then suddenly refuse the offer of a wall, which would offer not only protection, but peace of mind for people to go about their business without fear of attack?

BEYOND THE RED GAUNTLET

Stuart McCartney – Community Development Worker

Ardoyne Road Questions!

I find that when I look back to the events that took place on the days surrounding the protest, I discover that I am in a state of disbelief and have a mind full of unanswered questions. So much so, that it almost seems like I'm looking at a script for the X-files, with my mind shouting conspiracy and hidden agenda. But here are some of my coherent memories.

I'll never forget seeing the Police beating a small group of pensioners about their arms and legs with their batons while they were standing in their own garden; their own property. A property they had more right to be on than the police. My questions are, what seemed so threatening about them, that they had to be beaten; in what world is this action right and just?

I'll never forget seeing two Protestant women huddling over a pram to protect it while the police beat and pushed them. I could hear their screams "the pram, the pram, watch the pram," and before our eyes it was pushed over and the baby was thrown from it. At the same time I was struggling to help pull another pram out from under shields and booting feet with a young teenage girl. My own feelings were of helplessness as I watched it all, as if it was in slow motion replay. And I'll never forget having to make that decision, an unforgivable decision that they forced me to make; who should I help first? Help the two women with the pram or the 15-year old girl protecting hers from the same fate. It was a hateful choice to make!

I'll never forget trying to reason with the Police for 10 minutes; but was not even allowed to talk with the inspector in charge. I was being shoved back from the inspector, and told "the decision has been made." WHY? Because 12 people wanted to go to a Halloween party; People who had just walked down the Ardoyne Road 10 minutes before; WHY? Could they not have waited up at the school? Oh! I remember now, they were the only victims allowed to have rights implemented.

I'll never forget standing afterwards weeping at the side of the road. For what had just been done and for God knows what was to come.

I'll never forget the countless nights, now almost merged into one, where shots were fired and stones thrown. Whereas my community, was the only one occupied by a mass of security forces; the only one being beaten into their own streets. My Questions - why do the PSNI not police nationalist areas? What's the sense of policing Glenbryn if the gunman opened fire from Alliance Avenue? - Surely that is where they ought to be? But no this was Glenbryn and it was not news worthy or important to do the right thing for this community.

I'll never forget jumping in front of a Police land-rover to stop it as it mounted a pavement as it tried to scare a blind man off the road. You guessed it! They didn't see the stick! I took his hand and guided it to the bonnet of the vehicle to let him know how close he had come. I'll never forget seeing him beaten and dragged off, hidden from the media's eyes with shields with no thought to his disability. I'll never forget taking photo's of the house that was ransacked by the police, of the rooms turned upside down and the look of its helpless female owner. She told us of how the police eventually explained, "Sorry we got the wrong house"

What will I remember? I will remember a hostile nationalist community that did not want to negotiate, their lies on television and their insincere talk of dialogue and their hollow words of parity of esteem.

I will remember a provocative police force that did and still do, only police one side of a divided community - be it in Glenbryn or East Belfast.

I will remember press/media that refused to scratch below the surface; that didn't seem to know what investigative reporting was anymore. And how when the press/media did show the protest, it was always the worst days they re-ran. 4 fateful days out of 22 weeks of order, but that doesn't sell airtime does it? And how did they conveniently ignore the constant attacks that the community had to put up with.

I will remember silent politicians and the condemnations of the clergy instead of its ministry.

We have long memories and we will not forget!

But one final thing I will say, I believe I have stood beside some of the bravest people I will ever know, the salt of the earth. These people even though beaten, ignored, frustrated and misunderstood would not go down quietly, even in apparent defeat. We have long memories and we did not surrender to terrorism.

Chapter 14
Fourteen

Letters from the heart

"If I had to select one quality, one personal characteristic that I regard as being most highly correlated with success, whatever the field, I would pick the trait of persistence; Determination; The will to endure to the end, to get knocked down seventy times and get up off the floor saying, "Here comes number seventy-one!"

-- Richard M. Devos

This community has been knocked down so many times and has always lifted its head, persistent and determined to endure what may come its way! What follows in this chapter are letters, plea's from the heart which were sent out at different times to politicians, media and communities across the world as far as the USA - Plea's that were written at times of pure frustration of being ignored.

Written 13th June 2002
An Upper Ardoyne Resident's Plea!

To Whom It May Concern:

The Concerned Residents of Upper Ardoyne have over the past year tried to engage with both the Lower Ardoyne Community and the Office of the First Minister and Deputy First Minister of NI, to stop the sectarian attacks and acts of intimidation on the Upper Ardoyne Community and effectively give this community their right to live safely. Even though all the members of CRUA were put under a death threat by the INLA, they were still willing to engage with anyone who could make a difference for the good of their community. The campaign by Republicans to intimidate and harass the residents of upper Ardoyne and other North Belfast Interfaces has been taken to an all time low because now the NEW government (OFMDFM) have engaged the Upper Ardoyne Community under false pretences in a number of processes and allowed the outcomes to be vetoed by elements within Lower Ardoyne.

None of their major concerns have been taken on board and in fact in their latest document (after 7 months of discussions and compromise on the part of Upper Ardoyne) have not even recognised why the residents want an adequate community safety measure in place. They have confused the idea of a wall to protect 4 houses with the fact that this whole community is under attack and a measure is needed to break the line of sight between the two main trouble spots especially when young people engage in recreational rioting which then sadly leads to the whole community constantly caught helplessly up in conflict.

BEYOND THE RED GAUNTLET

The Office Of the First Minister and Deputy First Minister asked this community to call off a protest which was initiated because of constant attacks (including a murder of a young father in the area, a young man left needing psychiatric care and two men beaten and left unconscious on the Ardoyne Road) to engage in a process to deal with their major safety concerns. Since then this community has constantly compromised to find middle ground the main safety issues and get into immediate dialogue to work on the other serious community issues in the area.

Firstly this community wanted a solid brick wall across the Ardoyne Road to ensure they could live in safety and help Upper Ardoyne again become the vibrant community it once was, where people are not living in fear of their lives. This was compromised to be a Lanark Way style security gate which once again was turned down by the security minister who said their was no cross community support for it - (we needed to ask our attackers to agree to it).

Then OFMDFM officials suggested a road realignment with a wall and a chicane to totally remove the line of sight. This was changed to a road realignment with a wall to take in our concerns about the line of sight and protection of our whole community - but this was opposed due to the line of sight for parents from Holy Cross Girls School.

Once again taking concerns on board this community further compromised THEIR safety and feeling of security to enable finding the middle ground and changed plans to accommodate the parents concerns and opening up a line of sight up the Ardoyne Road but ensuring the Upper Ardoyne community's safety concerns were also addressed.
Since then we have been told through the latest document from OFMDFM that "Yes, the proposal does give Lower Ardoyne a line of sight from the Everton Centre side of the road but they want to be able to see from both sides of the road. Now this pathetic, childish excuse (I want to stand on

both sides of the road not just one) is being used to stop the safety measures going ahead. Don't people recognise that the principle of compromise is that you may not always get 100% of what you want? If this excuse is given credibility, then it will effectively open up the Ardoyne Road wider than it is now with only a small wall to protect 4 houses but the rest of our community will be susceptible to larger incursions into the area. This will also create an impossible task for security forces that have to police the interface in the times of conflict and serious rioting, so needing more units to separate rival crowds. Due to lack of resources this community have already been told "defend yourselves, we can't handle this" by the police on a number of occasions when there are large orchestrated attacks.

We are sending this letter to you so you can see that this community has moved and compromised throughout the past year and have taken on board reasonable objections or arguments to try to accommodate all sides BUT we cannot compromise any further with the safety of our community (not 4 houses). Where is our NEW future promised under the present Good Friday Agreement? Please help us to persuade the First Minister and the Deputy First Minister to remember that their process was to end a protest and deal with the safety concerns of those in Upper Ardoyne who felt the need to protest in the first place. No-one wants to go back to protest on the Ardoyne Road, a road which in actual fact is seen as the gateway to the attacks on our community. If the safety of the residents of this area cannot or will not be taken seriously does it leave people any alternative but to physically demonstrate against the denial of their Human Rights and the rejection of compromise?

Due to the feeble and unstructured attempt by OFMDFM to intervene and help a situation they have in fact left this community once again in total frustration, and with no alternatives, the main reasons the protest was initiated in June 2001! Please help us in any way you can and remember if the public decides that the only way left to them is to use their legal right to protest; then it is through the bungling and mishandling of this process and the empty promises and failed processes by the First and Deputy First Ministers of NI. This community has engaged in, contributed to and consistently compromised in processes for the past year, which have been thrown back in our faces through lack of commitment and determination to adequately resolve the REAL Issues.

WHEN MEETING YOUR COUNTERPART HALFWAY IS NOT GOOD ENOUGH, WHAT IS THE POINT IN TALKING TO THEM?

Written 19th August 2002

Dear Friends

As I write this message, many Protestant families have already moved out of the Glenbryn area having taken enough of a second-class 'stranger-in-your-own-land' existence. Who cares? Residents of the normally stable Hesketh area beside Glenbryn are now starting to move out too, including a 70 year old pensioner, and a blind resident and his family who moved out over the weekend. Who cares? On Friday, Hesketh homes were attacked whilst PSNI officers were chatting to Nationalist community representatives only 30 feet away. Who cares? Our community house on Ardoyne Road was paint-bombed on Friday, Saturday and Sunday consecutively, under the nose of the CCTV cameras. Who cares? Our residents are back to facing up to the reality that we cannot travel along Crumlin Road at Ardoyne without being attacked (as I was again on Sunday night) again under the nose of the CCTV cameras. Perhaps Sinn Fein has persuaded the NIO to switch them off. Who cares?

PSNI are telling us that whilst they are in houses in Glenbryn watching Nationalists attack our homes, Nationalists are on the phone to them saying it is their homes being attacked - consequently the statistics show that there is an inflated number of attacks on Nationalist homes. This is of course deliberate so that the Security Minister's response is ill-informed and directed against those who are in fact being systematically beaten and shot out of their homes. It adds insult to injury, but who cares?

Whilst local elected representatives (MP, some councillors and MLA's) have worked themselves to the bone to try and help us, I have to ask if the rest of their colleagues even care enough to take a closer look at what is really happening, and not content themselves with digesting what they see on the news. The evidence is not encouraging. I have to ask myself, if Nationalists were moving out of their homes in such large numbers, would one or two Nationalist representatives turn up to highlight it? Certainly not - they would be there in force and every one of them would be highlighting the issue at every opportunity.

Does anyone appreciate the sheer scale of the numbers queuing up to get out of Upper Ardoyne? They are not going because they are easily frightened, or because they want an ideal existence. They are going because there is no prospect that their lives will change until Unionists all over the country, not just North Belfast, join in support to stop the march towards a Nationalist-only North Belfast. What happened on the City-side of Londonderry was bad enough, but those in power today are the same people who are letting it happen again in North Belfast. When I ask 'who cares' I know what the answer is as things stand at present. Is there someone out there who can do something so that if I ask the same question in 2 or 3 weeks time, the answer will be different? We will see.

Yours in total frustration
Mark Coulter

Chapter 15
Fifteen

Short Quotations...

BEYOND THE RED GAUNTLET

The following are some quotations that I have found throughout the years and can relate them to what happens or needs to happen in Upper Ardoyne or in fact North Belfast. The communities we have spoken about in this book have been mainly Protestant minorities in North Belfast............

> "The most certain test by which we judge whether a country is really free is the amount of security enjoyed by minorities."
> - Lord John Emerich Edward Dalberg Acton (1834-1902),
> British historian

Obviously this book has outlined the insecurities felt by the minority Protestant communities of North Belfast. If its people cannot live within their communities with relative security of person and possessions; then we most certainly are not a country that is really free; we are besieged by the hand of our own government in its failure to protect us.
- AB

> "What is a minority? The chosen heroes of this earth have been in a minority. There is not a social, political, or religious privilege that you enjoy today that was not bought for you by the blood and tears and patient suffering of the minority. It is the minority that have stood in the van of every moral conflict, and achieved all that is noble in the history of the world."
> -- John B. Gough

The minority community of Upper Ardoyne have stood suffering patiently with blood, sweat and tears to try to achieve the privilege of living in a safe community without intimidation. Although critically cut down in front of the world, they have stood by their morals throughout the history of this conflict. They are my chosen heroes!
-AB

"Endurance is one of the most difficult disciplines, but it is to the one who endures that the final victory comes."
- Buddha (563?-483? BC), [Siddhartha Gautama]
Indian mystic, founder of Buddhism

The Communities of North Belfast have endured attacks, intimidation, loss of life, severe housing conditions, high unemployment, low educational attainment - I pray that their final victory will come when they can live in peace and safety.
- AB

It is easy to be brave from a safe distance
- AESOP (620 - 560 BC)

Take heed, Mr Blair, Mr Trimble and Mr Durkan, you cannot feel the hurt and pain these communities are going through; you do not have to endure it, but you should empathise and recognise it as genuine; and acknowledge their fears as though they were your own!
- AB

"Falsehood is easy, truth so difficult."
-- George Eliot (1819-80)

Throughout the "troubles" in Northern Ireland there have been many purposeful falsehoods and still they continue to this day. These are followed by the recriminations of the "blame game". Lets dismiss the easy and strive to accomplish the difficult - genuineness and truth!
- AB

"A pessimist sees the difficulty in every opportunity; an optimist sees the opportunity in every difficulty."
-Sir Winston Leonard Spenser Churchill (1874-1965),
British statesman, prime minister

So many people have to tolerate the difficulties in North Belfast and are prevented from the chance of opportunity. This is until a safe environment is created to enable them. We All must endeavour to continue looking for the positives in our community and build on them; to create an optimistic future for our children and our communities.
- AB

"Always remember that striving and struggle precede success, even in the dictionary."
- Sarah Ban Breathnach

The Upper Ardoyne Community been striving to survive; they have struggled to have the truth heard; surely they deserve to have success in achieving safety in their community!
- AB

BEYOND THE RED GAUNTLET

··· Author's Note

• • •

Doomed Twofold - Sectarian wrath combines with political incompetence to wreak havoc on a chronically beleaguered people.... The worst way to show this Community progress was to condemn it!

Sadly the whole district of North Belfast is a deeply divided patchwork area. Living in North Belfast for most of my life, I am not naive enough to believe that the whole of Ireland are out to persecute Protestants and especially those in Interface areas. But I must say I have had my eyes opened over the past 15 months to the treacherous dirty dealings of government, security forces and Republicanism.

Working in a local flashpoint area for over 20 years, I believed had given me a generous wealth of experience of life in North Belfast. But nothing could have prepared me for the appalling scenes, betrayals and belligerence that I have witnessed over these months.

I have watched as a community responded to low-key and murderous attacks, as they came from being an apathetic, segregated, frustrated, degenerated, neighbourhood who felt they could do nothing but tolerate all the world was throwing at them, to becoming a district who stood against all the odds to try as best they could to highlight the artificial and deceitful falsehoods being portrayed against their community.

If through reading this account of events you make the decision that the Upper Ardoyne Community genuinely took action to highlight their need for community safety, or if you choose to believe that those who were involved in the action are sectarian thugs, then at least I know you have made this decision through an informed choice; where you have been given some of the factual information surrounding the events and history of this area and not just been left to the mainly biased spiel of the media and Republicans; I will only then have fulfilled my objective for writing this sequence of events.

Anne.

BEYOND THE RED GAUNTLET

BEYOND THE RED GAUNTLET

BEYOND THE RED GAUNTLET